D0467622

Morgan just has a way! *Peace Is a Practice* is a thoughtful, Spirit-led call to action. This book lets you know that peace is possible!

MICHELLE WILLIAMS, speaker, singer, and author of *Checking In*

Morgan's new book is not only a beautiful piece of art to look at but is also packed with such helpful advice and words of wisdom. I have found so much comfort and joy in this book. Morgan has a gift with words: she knows exactly what needs to be said and how it should be said. It is truly a masterpiece!

DR. CAROLINE LEAF, neuroscientist, mental health expert, bestselling author, and podcast host of *Cleaning Up Your Mental Mess*

I'm so inspired by Morgan every day. Her words speak to me gently yet hold me accountable at the same time.

HOLLY ROBINSON PEETE, actor, author, and philanthropist

Both challenge and invitation, *Peace Is a Practice* beckons to the very core of our humanity and, in the most intentionally beautiful way, breathes life and hope back into our collective soul.

KENNESHA BUYCKS, creative, speaker, and author of *Restoration House*

These stories and practices possess both a honed vulnerability and a depth of contemplation that are truly refreshing. Morgan is forming each of us into a spiritual creative, connected to our breath, our body, and our own interior world in a way that offers the peace and healing we were meant for.

COLE ARTHUR RILEY, author of *This Here Flesh*

PEACE IS A PRACTICE

An Invitation to Breathe Deep
and Find a New Rhythm for Life

MORGAN HARPER NICHOLS

ZONDERVAN BOOKS

ZONDERVAN BOOKS

Peace Is a Practice
Copyright © 2022 by Morgan Harper Nichols

Requests for information should be addressed to:
Zondervan, *3900 Sparks Dr. SE, Grand Rapids, Michigan 49546*

Zondervan titles may be purchased in bulk for educational, business, fundraising, or
sales promotional use. For information, please email SpecialMarkets@Zondervan.com.

ISBN 978-0-310-36170-1 (hardcover)
ISBN 978-0-310-36173-2 (audio)
ISBN 978-0-310-36172-5 (ebook)

Cover design: Morgan Harper Nichols
Cover illustration: Morgan Harper Nichols
Interior design: Denise Froehlich
Interior illustrations: Morgan Harper Nichols

Printed in the United States of America

21 22 23 24 25 26   /LSC/   10 9 8 7 6 5 4 3 2 1

To my family

CONTENTS

PREFACE

For most of my life, I lived with undiagnosed autism.

I spent years living with a struggle without a name. Throughout daily life, a pendulum in my mind swung back and forth between these two thoughts: "I think there's something wrong with me, and I need to figure out what to do with myself," and, "I think something's wrong with me, and I need help . . ."

When I was twenty-seven, I finally had just enough courage to ask my primary care doctor for advice on pursuing an autism diagnosis.

Throughout my childhood, my parents had wondered if I might be on the autism spectrum, but after asking doctors over the years, they were told there was nothing to worry about. I would later find out that most of the studies on autism have been done with boys, so sometimes girls have an incredibly hard time getting support in pursuit of an autism diagnosis.

As I sat there under the blinking fluorescent light, slowly lifting my gaze from the brown tile floor, I finally let out the words, "Do you have any suggestions for who I could talk to about autism spectrum disorder? I think I could be on the spectrum."

Without even looking up from his clipboard, my doctor spouted out confidently, "You have nothing to worry about. You're perfectly normal."

Sadly, I left that room believing him. The pendulum in my mind swung back again: "I guess I need to figure this out myself." I spent the next few years trying to do just that.

It wasn't until years later that I discovered videos of women talking about their experiences with getting diagnosed with autism as adults. I sat there in awe as I listened. I felt as though they were describing my whole life. Through those videos, I found the courage to seek help again. I ended up finding a specialist in my area and was finally able to talk to someone for the first time.

Autism spectrum disorder is a developmental disorder, and the range of symptoms varies widely. The word *spectrum* is important when it comes to autism because it looks different person to person. Signs of autism begin during early childhood and typically last throughout adulthood. Autism can affect everything in daily life, from how someone socializes and communicates to how they learn and function. My own diagnosis includes a sensory processing disorder, which in my case means something as simple as the texture of clothing or a bright light can have a profound impact on me and my ability to process and be present in the moment.

For years I have been incredibly hard on myself for having these sensitivities. When I was a touring musician, sometimes I would walk off stage ready to cry and didn't know why. I felt overwhelmed physically, even when I felt fine emotionally. Now I've realized that the high volume from the massive speakers and the sound of all the instruments was wearing me down minute by minute.

My life has been filled with stories like this. From as early as I can remember all the way into being an adult, I have had moments when I felt ready to shut down, but I had no idea why. Moments when I would go into a bathroom and sit in the stall just to have a moment of silence. Moments when I would run and hide and retreat to a dark place just to get my heart rate down.

I would also have moments when I would go outside and just stare at the wide-open sky.

I would sit on the front porch of my childhood home and carefully observe the rocks scattered around my feet.

I would go to the nearest pine tree and grab hold of the bark and just stand there for a while.

I would pull out my sketchbook and doodle my way into the margins.

I would sit at the kitchen table and scribble out poetry.

I would sing.

I would practice peace.

When the specialist officially gave me my diagnosis, which was rather long and was certainly a lot to take in, the last thing she said was, "And it's not your fault."

Before she came into the room, I had been gripping the pillow on the couch the entire time. As she said those words, I loosened my grip, and with this loosened grip came at least a decade's worth of tears. For so long I had struggled with everyday tasks that I felt I should be able to do. I had told myself it was all on me to manage the daily stresses and anxieties I faced. Somewhere along the way, I had decided to carry the weight of everything I struggled with on my shoulders. Every friendship I had struggled to maintain. Every job I struggled to keep. Every social situation where I had to plan out topics in advance only to walk away feeling like I didn't say what I meant to. Every time I struggled to be present in a group of people. But now I was seeing my struggles differently. Yes, I struggled . . . and it was okay. I didn't have to carry it all. I didn't have to hold it all in.

I also discovered as I looked back over my life, even though it was hard to see it at the time, I breathed through all those difficult moments, one inhale, one exhale at a time. Over and over, through the mountains and valleys of my life, I made my way through breath cycles, too many to count. The challenges I face made it difficult to be in the moment, and at the same time, I learned that just being able to breathe was a way into peace . . . and this was a miraculous thing.

From the hopeful blueness of the sky, to the strength of the pine tree's bark, to the blank pages that invited me to fill them after a long day—these were ways that, while I struggled, I also learned to breathe. While I was trying to pace myself through the unknown, I was also practicing peace.

CHAPTER 1

PEACE IS A PRACTICE

The word *peace* first caught my attention as a child when I heard the song "It Is Well with My Soul."

> When peace like a river, attendeth my way,
> When sorrows like sea billows roll;
> Whatever my lot, thou hast taught me to say,
> It is well, it is well, with my soul.

From that moment forward, I associated the word *peace* with a river, a beautiful yet powerful watercourse I had never seen with my own eyes, but it was a place I longed for. Because I struggled to fit in and feel at home in the world around me, the idea of peace drew me in. I was hungry for the green leaves that sheltered the river and thirsty for the water that flowed throughout. When I learned the story behind the song, my association deepened even more.

Horatio Spafford's four daughters died in a shipwreck while crossing the Atlantic. When he crossed the same ocean to join his grieving wife, who had survived the wreck, he penned the words to this song.

He had known peace to be like a river in his life, and sorrows to be like the sea. He had known more than one body of water. And for him, they meant different things.

As a young girl, I too associated the sea with sorrow. I learned of the slave trade that brought my ancestors over the Atlantic. The architectural plans in history books of their bodies lined up below the deck created a lump in my throat. If slaves grew ill or did not comply with the enslaver in some way, they were thrown overboard to their death. My stomach tightened at this knowledge. I still can't look to the Atlantic Ocean without thinking of them.

In contrast, the river was a symbol of freedom and peace for my soul. I could feel this meaning in the Negro spirituals I sang as a child. All by grace, these songs have survived and traveled down through the generations. Through years of enslavement and relentless oppression, songs like "Deep River" became a part of the tradition:

> *Deep river, my home is over Jordan . . .*
> *Oh, don't you want to go to that gospel feast,*
> *That promised land where all is peace?*[1]

The author of this song, and many others like it, remains unknown. I don't have the privilege of knowing the authors' individual stories. But I can feel the collective longing for peace beneath my skin, generations later.

As the song suggests, "peace" still exists within the question mark, not on the other side. Questions about justice, safety, healing, hope. Questions that make us wonder, "Will we ever be truly free?"

We're still desperate to reach that deep river. We're still desperate for peace.

Peace is a state of mind, heart, body, and soul. It is the freedom to breathe, even in the face of great challenges and chaos. Peace is the river in the desert, not on the other side of it.

Today I am still seeking that river. And not just a river far off somewhere that I must arrive at, but the river that runs wild and free in my inner life. The river that carves its way through my need for understanding and reminds me to slow down and breathe.

My senses strive for the smallest taste of peace in the morning's dewy air. The steam lifting above poured tea. The way the house settles back into place after a freight train rolls by. Why? Because it is precisely that moment in the day when I return to the present moment. It is there I realize that when the walls shake, the ground is still steady beneath. My body finds the resolve it naturally seeks.

These are small things, yes, but in times lined with uncertainty, they remind me of the bigger things. They remind me that I can be aware of this very moment, no matter my fears of the future and no matter what I am wrestling from the past.

I am free to slow down long enough to reflect on what is true. I don't know what lies ahead, but I stand on the shoulders of those who came before me. The strength of my great-great-grandfather who was born a slave and died free. My parents, who taught me to sing songs of peace. The painters and poets who created openly and widely, never knowing of me. The teenage girl transformed by what they made—quietly taking in their work as I stood in the narrow gaps between the shelves at the local library. It was in that small space that I found freedom to breathe.

This is what peace means to me.

I have played around with the phrases *finding peace* and *seeking peace* and *peace beyond understanding* in my art and poetry. And not just because they fit nicely. I hope that for whoever is on the other side of that phrase, it reminds them to exhale, right in the middle of the uncertainty. For even when we haven't yet seen the other side of the issues we're facing, we are still worthy of breathing deep and knowing peace right here amid them.

I write this way because I am desperate for peace. And I have a feeling you might be too.

This book is about learning to seek peace in daily life. It's about realizing we are worthy of peace. And it starts right here: with a deep inhale and a hold-nothing-back exhale as you ground yourself in the grace of the present. You don't have to arrive at your picture-perfect life before you can know peace. The river is here for you now, wherever you are.

I believe grasping peace is important because, more and more, I feel the tension rising. And you probably feel it too. We are thirsty for the river and hungry for the fruit that grows around its bend, but all around and within, all we see are floodwaters. Everything seems to tremble with chaos.

What new problems will rise to the surface today?

What will the headlines read?

What systems and structures are failing vulnerable people?

Who can we trust?

A lot is being uncovered right now. Can't we just get it all out of the way? Can't we just have all the difficult conversations we need to have right now? Will there come a time when we are able to experience one big exhale and that's enough? Will we finally see real change? Will we experience peace collectively?

And then there are all the questions you're holding within. You're trying to figure out how to breathe through all the uncertainty. You're trying to learn how to be present amid the tension. You want to say what your heart wants to say, but is that safe? You want to find the courage to be fully present to others and to love them well, but will that be enough? You feel a stirring inside you to take up space, but in an anxious world, is that okay?

Often it seems where one part of the world is calm, something is shaken up in another. When you feel content and joyful, you check in with a friend, and she is anxious and overwhelmed. You fix one thing, and something else falls apart. You sit down for a meal and try to forget everything for a moment, but the weight of all that happened that day is as strong as an earthquake. It rocks the ceiling, the floor, the cups, and the plates. It creates tsunamis, physical ones and inner ones. Everything gets shaken up. Suffering is widespread. Fear boils in the underbelly of conversations with your relatives and the ones you have with yourself. You wonder when the volcano will finally erupt. You wonder, "Where is the river?"

What I have learned in writing poetry and making art about peace over the past few years is that peace is a practice. The word *practice* means "to carry out," and peace is a way of living that we can carry out each day—maybe not everywhere all at once, but we can learn to find peace and live in its presence.

The people who came before us faced many troubles. And yet they continued to sing, march, dance, cook, nurture, vote, and create. We can practice living in the same way. We can contribute to the flow. We don't have to figure it out all at once to know we are free. Free to approach each day being present with every breath we breathe, every word we speak. We have the opportunity to sow seeds of life and water them daily. We can practice peace.

I have also learned that peace does not mean the annihilation of discomfort. Peace is not complicit or passive. As sure as you can hear a mighty river rushing from miles away, peace roars its cry for justice. Peace is a constant flow of sacred truth. "Blessed are the peacemakers" (Matthew 5:9)—humbling, eternal words, carved through the wild, centuries after they were spoken. Peace is an invitation in daily life to breathe deep, right here, in the uncertainty.

PEACE IS A PRACTICE

Breathe free.
Through complicated histories
and deeply rooted mysteries,
let us practice peace.
Let us live it out day by day, breath by breath.
Peace:
above, beneath, all around, and within.
Let us pursue peace, together,
for the living, breathing flow that it is.

If nothing else, I hope this book encourages you to pursue peace right here, right now. I hope you leave this book having cultivated an imagination for what peace looks like in daily life. It is my hope that in the spaces where you hunger for justice, you can sow seeds of restoration. Where you thirst for answers, you can drink of calm waters. Where your whole being craves a resolve, each breath you breathe reminds you of the path beneath your feet. And not every breath has to be perfect. The river does not flow in a straight line, and the current is prone to change. But the water still flows. And you are free to practice peace.

Peace is a river that the soul longs for.

Peace is also a practice available to us, right here, in everyday life.

PEACE IS A PRACTICE

Late one summer my family traveled a few hours south to Savannah, Georgia, where we visited the historical First African Baptist Church, which is also a museum. The sun beamed brightly above us, and the August humidity sent me rushing to get indoors. As I reached the top of the steps, out of breath, and opened the red door, I immediately knew something was different about this place. The lights were off and the air was cool. The sanctuary was quiet as the tour guide led our group to the basement. Here I learned that "beneath the wooden floor, builders left a space four feet tall, large enough to hide hundreds of slaves following the Savannah River to freedom. They punctured holes in the floor in the cross-and-diamond shape of an African prayer symbol."[2]

This would have occurred during the time of the Underground Railroad, a network of people working to create secret and safe pathways for runaway slaves to escape to freedom, and "it is believed that the drilled pattern functioned as breathing holes for runaway slaves who, hiding under the floor, awaited safe transport north."[3]

For the runaway slave in the South, the mere act of breathing in the wrong place was a death sentence.

I stood there, suddenly hyperaware of the deep breaths I was free to take. I tried to imagine what it might be like to try to breathe through the centuries-old holes drilled beneath my feet, my body pressed against others, eager to be free, knowing that because I was in a Black body, my freedom was a crime. Unlike the railroad up the street from my house, I'm sure that the Underground Railroad would have been something I was grateful for. But still, there had to be moments when the weight of it all was too much. My shoulders tensed up at the thought of how these small holes in the floor didn't seem like enough room to breathe.

Our tour guide shared knowledge with us that you can also find on the "History" section of the First African Baptist Church's website: "The holes in the floor are in the shape of an African prayer symbol known to some as the BaKongo Cosmogram. In parts of Africa, it also means 'Flash of the Spirits' and represents birth, life, death, and rebirth."[4]

Rebirth.

I let the word rise like its own miniature sunrise on my tongue. My shoulders loosened ever so slightly. They loosened at the reality that amid all the uncertainty these slaves faced, they looked up and saw something familiar. I was reminded of Monica A. Coleman's words on rebirth in her book *Bipolar Faith*: "My rebirths are not as dramatic as in human biology. . . . I feel it internally, like snapping a twig underfoot on a nature hike or the sunrise turning from orange to pink. . . . Rebirth is the surety that I am more than this. I am more than this. I am more than this."[5]

These slaves had no idea what their tomorrow held, and yet, in the smallest way, there was breathing room. Every exhale, an act of faith all on its own. *"There is more than this."*

To practice peace is to take action. To practice peace is to drill breathing holes in the church floor for those seeking freedom. It is to look for ceremonial pauses between a song's verses. It is to let ourselves be present when the windows shake and the train rolls by. Over and over again. It is realizing that life is not about fixing or solving problems on our own. We are connected to a larger, greater network, and the best way forward is to stay focused to work we can do together. And we can take action by asking ourselves questions like these:

What can I learn right here?
What can I pay attention to right now?
What invitations are disguised as interruptions?

Even if we can't fix life's challenges all at once, we can create breathing room, a new way of life.

There is peace to be found.

And it starts not in our heads but right here, on the ground.

PRACTICE
IS A
CYCLE

CHAPTER 2

PRACTICE IS A CYCLE

THE PRACTICE CYCLE

When I was a young driver living in Atlanta, Georgia, many times parallel parking was the only option downtown. Because I was (and still am) terrible at parallel parking, it would take me a long time to maneuver my way into the spot. So whenever another car came up behind me while I was trying to wiggle into a space, I would back out of the space and circle around the block and try again. I would do this countless times until I finally got it right. In the moment, I felt like I was wasting time, but looking back, I was practicing.

Practice is coming back to something over and over, even when we feel like we're failing. While I am still not great at parallel parking, I am now unashamed of circling the block if I need to. In the same way, to practice peace, we have to be willing to fail and try again.

Whether or not we feel like we are good at what we do, we are all practicing every day, circling back to the same tasks and information over and over again, learning something new every time. When an athlete wins a game, they go back to practice the next day. One patient can open a seasoned doctor's eyes to something new. And a teacher learns alongside their students each year.

It is through practice that we learn what we're capable of. We learn to distribute our energy and minimize burnout. We learn when to stop and when to go. Through practice, we learn to pace ourselves. We learn to make room for repetition. We learn to keep coming back to what matters. We learn to accept that as long as we are living, this is something we will always have to do if we want to improve.

Practice is necessary for growth, but you may not always notice how necessary it is in real time. Practicing peace is no different. When you take deep breaths before having a conversation, you may not feel like you are practicing peace, but you are. You practice peace all the time, and the more you are mindful of it, the more you will continue to grow.

THE BREATH CYCLE

An incredibly important, and often overlooked, part of practicing peace is simply breathing.

I first learned to pay attention to my breathing in the pink-tiled bathroom between my sister's and my bedrooms of our childhood home. That's where the "breathing machine" was. We both had asthma, and every night before bed, my parents would help us take turns using the nebulizer machine that turned liquid medicine into mist to help us breathe.

I don't know the exact number of nights I had to end the day with the nebulizer machine, but I do know it wasn't one and done. I had to return to this place at the end of each day and repeatedly focus on nothing but breathing. Of course I wouldn't have called this a "practice" back then, but this routine taught me that no matter what I experience in a specific day, even if I work around the clock, at some point I still need to do nothing more than focus on my breath cycle. The same is true for you. No need to run around and prove that you can breathe just fine. No need to recount every other breath you took that day. Just sit there and breathe, over and over again, and that's enough.

But just working through the breath cycle doesn't always feel like it's enough.

We often speak in language that paints a portrait of life as linear and upward. If someone is becoming more successful, they're "moving on up." If someone marries someone of an elite socioeconomic class, they "married up." And while we do "grow up" into adulthood and "stand up" for what's right, a lot of life looks more like a cycle.

The act of breathing in is called inhalation. Breathing out is called exhalation. Together, one inhale and one exhale complete a respiratory cycle, and then we repeat this cycle over and over, all day. Inhaling and exhaling are undoubtedly vital to life, but as we get older, many of us forget how to breathe properly. According to Harvard Health Publishing, even the stresses of everyday life can cause us to "gradually shift to shallower, less satisfying 'chest breathing.'"[1] Breathing deeply is something we have to relearn how to do because "shallow breathing limits the diaphragm's range of motion. The lowest part of the lungs doesn't get a full share of oxygenated air. That can make you feel short of breath and anxious."[2]

In contrast, "Deep abdominal breathing encourages full oxygen exchange. . . . This type of breathing slows the heartbeat and can lower or stabilize blood pressure."[3]

In an article in the *Wall Street Journal*, James Nestor, author of *Breath: The New Science of a Lost Art*, provides research and practices on proper breathing: "The first step in healthy breathing: extending breaths to make them a little deeper, a little longer. . . . When we breathe like this we can better protect the lungs from irritation and infection while boosting circulation to the brain and body. Stress on the heart relaxes; the respiratory and nervous systems enter a state of coherence where everything functions at peak efficiency. Just a few minutes of inhaling and exhaling at this pace can drop blood pressure by 10, even 15 points."[4]

This information is nothing new—it's just that we easily and quickly forget. The more we look back, the more we will be reminded that breathing has always been foundational. And when we feel lost, we are free to come back to the breath. This is how we come alive.

Learning to breathe deeply, fully, and from my belly is something my body is still learning. It is a practice that modern life distracts me from but one I am committed to. It is a wisdom I will humbly approach.

I learned the importance of breathing deeply a few years ago when I took my first real hike. As I traveled along the Bell Trail toward the "Crack" at Wet Beaver Creek in Rimrock, Arizona, I was reminded of the importance of breathing properly. Because there weren't exactly any signs that said, "Welcome, First-Timers! Please remember to breathe," I had to learn the hard way. As I walked, the elevation increased, making it even harder to get the oxygen I needed. I had to learn to stop and take mindful inhales and exhales. It wasn't until I learned to take deep breaths that I was able to successfully reach the end of the trail.

The value of a deep breath is something we must continue to learn and relearn on the path to peace, exchanging our quick, shallow breaths for a cycle of breath that represents the fullness of how we were meant to breathe—mindfully, wholly.

I have written quite a bit of poetry about taking a moment to breathe, which has caused me to think about why it's so hard to remember to take those long, slow inhales and exhales throughout the day. Now, I'm no scientist, but I wonder if the reason why this concept is difficult to grasp is because our breath isn't something we can just hold in our hands. It's hard for us humans to fully conceptualize and realize the importance of what we can't hold.

In this way, "breath" is similar to the word "wind" in ancient Hebrew. *Breath* can also mean "wind" or "spirit." This is what breathes life and animates dry bones. Breath is more than just the inhales and exhales that leave our bodies. Breath is a force, connecting us to life.

To see the importance of mindful breathing, we have to think of our inhales and exhales as something bigger than us. We have to see our breath as something that not only keeps us alive but also links us to all other life. It's what connects us to everything from the ground beneath our feet to people we interact with each day.

From the moment life is breathed into us, to inhale and exhale is to complete this small yet meaningful cycle that reminds us of what we need to do to live: to take in and let out.

The Inhale

Inhaling is the act of taking it all in. It's making room for inspiration.

Inspiration is another word for "inhalation" in the medical sense, as it relates to the respiratory system. When air enters the lungs, this ventilation phase is called inspiration.[5]

As an artist, I can't resist the artistic connotations here. I am often asked where I find my inspiration for poetry and art. I can honestly tell you it's on the inhale. It's that incoming flow. Inspiration isn't about what we're gathering together and putting out. Inspiration is about what we're taking in.

I find inspiration as I breathe deep and take in the world around me. Even when I'm not consciously thinking about it, I am taking in my environment. And then, as I sit down to write, the words that come to me are from all the experiences I've had that day and the story I've already lived.

But to fill the page and to pour out, I must first open myself up to inhale it all. I openly witness everything around me, allowing my senses to experience the world fully, what I can see, hear, smell, taste, and touch. And furthermore, I don't try to make sense of it all right away.

Now that I understand the issues I deal with on a sensory level, this step has been incredibly important. Music often seems louder to me than it is to others. The air conditioning blows the weight of a cold day's wind. I have to take deep breaths to make it through many moments. But at the same time, this sensitivity has taught me how to pay attention. How to notice. How to listen. How to take in.

Sometimes inhaling just looks like listening. In her essay "The Reader as Artist," Toni Morrison said this:

> Listening required me to surrender to the narrator's world while remaining alert inside it. That Alice-in-Wonderland combination of willing acceptance coupled with intense inquiry is still the way I read literature: slowly, digging for the hidden, questioning or relishing the choices the author made, eager to envision what is there, noticing what is not. In listening and in reading, it is when I surrender to the language, enter it, that I see clearly. Yet only if I remain attentive to its choices can I understand deeply. Sometimes the experience is profound, harrowing, beautiful; other times enraging, contemptible, unrewarding. Whatever the consequence, the practice itself is riveting. I don't need to "like" the work; I want instead to "think" it.[6]

Let the practice itself be riveting. Sometimes you will read something and find exactly what you were hoping for, and sometimes you will be wildly disappointed. Sometimes you'll pack the car and drive out to the ocean fully anticipating settling down on the gritty brown sand and taking in the salty air, but it ends up raining and you have to go back home. Take it in. All of it.

A lot of what I inhale, a lot of the beauty of which I breathe deeply, I don't ever end up writing about. Many thoughts I keep sacred. They are private, written in my journal, or shared among close friends. We shouldn't inhale with the anticipation that everything we take in will someday turn into a product or a poem. Some things maybe we are just meant to take in for now, and that alone is enough.

The Exhale

Exhaling is the realization that when I let go of all that is inside me, I find freedom. There is freedom in letting go. To exhale is a form of release. It is so much better to let the tension out of our bodies, to release it and experience this freedom, than it is to keep it pent up and churning inside. To exhale is to say:

> I've done the work I can do.
> I've taken in what I can take in.
> Now is the time to release. Let it go.
> Before I repeat this process again.

To practice the exhale is to practice letting go, moment by moment. Surrender is a practice too, and some questions take months to answer. Some books will take decades to write. Some wounds take years to heal. But deep down in the fullness of your own belly, you know this. Your body knows that you're free to breathe through the process as you wait to see how everything comes together.

You're free to invite someone over for dinner before the kitchen table is photo ready. You're free to finish the workday with a few emails left unanswered. You're free to be generous with your time without knowing what the future holds. You're free to exhale, knowing you have a long way to go on this road.

> Inhale. Exhale. Let this be your practice.
> Complete this cycle over and over.
> Let it be a reminder of your body, mind, heart,
>   and soul's need
> for wholeness over perfection,
> and peace.

THE TIME CYCLE

A sundial was an ancient tool used to tell time. A solid pin or rod was placed upward on a circular stone plate. When sunlight hit the rod, it would cast a shadow to let you know what time of day it was. The shadow would move with the sun and become invisible at high noon. This instrument was an important development in our current understanding of time, and looking at the design of an analog clock, you'll see traces of how this discovery has played out over time.

As a kid I was never particularly swift at telling time, learning the ways of the analog clock. I am first to say I am grateful for digital clocks so I no longer have to struggle to figure out what time it is. But I also think we may be losing something by getting rid of clocks with a circular motion.

I don't want to be too philosophical here, but I think that as much as we may crave clarity so that we can move forward, we have to remember the circular nature of this life we live. Yes, we get older each day, but the sun that shines today will be the same one that shines tomorrow. No two sunrises are the same, but it is in fact the same sun. No two days are exactly the same, but it is in fact the same life—a life where, even as we experience change, the ground is still steady beneath our feet. Light still finds us. Shadows find us too.

Seasons are cyclical too. One of the reasons why we often feel stuck in a loop is because in many ways, in life, we are in an actual loop. Even though every day is different, we go through cycles of life in the same way we cycle through nature's seasons. Even though no two winters are exactly the same, we come to know winter every year. In *Wintering*, Katherine May writes, "Life meanders like a path through the woods. We have seasons when we flourish and seasons when the leaves fall from us, revealing our bare bones. Given time, they grow again."[7]

Every single day, we work through the exciting and the mundane and every moment in between, one minute at a time. The sunlight still finds us, even as we make our way down the same hallways each day. Sunlight still finds us, even as we go to the same jobs and deal with variations of the same problems every day. We learn to love and to say goodbye, and we learn to grow and to wait, season after season.

THE STORY CYCLE

When I was a kid, I was obsessed with the 1995 film *It Takes Two*. I watched it so often that I had it fully memorized, and even watching it as an adult, I can still quote entire chunks of this movie. There's something comforting about watching a movie over and over. You have the satisfaction of knowing how it ends, but by watching it again and again, you can engage in the delight of how it all begins. I think there's a reason many of us want to watch the same movies and shows repeatedly. In a world that feels uncertain, it's comforting to know how a story ends.

The concept of the hero's journey, popularized by Joseph Campbell, maps out a character's story arc from beginning to end. I love this concept, but when you watch a movie or listen to a story, you get only one story cycle of the many story cycles in the character's life. It's like when the romantic comedy ends at the wedding, or the action film ends with defeating the villain. We don't see what happens after the wedding or get introduced to the next villain. We think of our stories as linear, but they actually happen as cycles.

In her book *The Heroine's Journey*, therapist Maureen Murdock offers a model of the traditional "hero's journey" for her female patients. For this version of the journey, she notes, "Movement through the stages of the journey is cyclic, and a person may be at several stages of the journey at one time."[8]

Many versions of "the journey" are out there, but one element that many of them have in common is a part of the cycle that includes the character encountering death. This could be about losing a loved one or experiencing life-altering betrayal or suffering an illness.

While a movie might focus on one death, in real life we encounter many losses, and we're even affected when those we love experience their own losses. We cycle through loss and are present to others as they cycle through it as well. Perhaps this is why our stresses and anxieties never end. We sit at the edge of one loss having to worry about when the next one will come. We are forever cycling through. The good news is that we also cycle through moments of joy, meaningful connection, divine encounters with love, and healing.

Seeing our stories as part of a cycle reminds us that we go in and out of life experiences just like we breathe in and out. So when we don't know what to do, perhaps the best thing to do is breathe through. To recognize that even if we can't name it, every experience is a part of a cycle.

Remember, practice is coming back to something over and over, learning as we go. This is how we grow. So here's to using our breath cycle to enter into our practicing cycle so that we are equipped for the cycles of life.

Breathe.

Practice.

Live life to the full.

SHADOW
AND
LIGHT

CHAPTER 3

SHADOW AND LIGHT

Practicing peace is learning to be present in the moment. So what do you do with all the emotions and thoughts that arise? If the moment is filled with the tension of both shadow and light, how can we find peace there? In moments of stillness, when you are faced with both the good and the bad, how do you hold the tension of everything coming your way?

When I was just shy of two years old, one evening my parents took me to look at Christmas lights. As we drove down the streets of multiple neighborhoods, they pointed out the fully decked-out homes, saying, "Morgan, look at the lights!" I followed their lead, pointing at every house that contained Christmas lights, exclaiming, "Light! Light! Light!"

But it didn't stop there. My parents told me that on the way home, I was equally entranced by every other light I saw. The lights at the gas station. The traffic lights. The yellow glow from the McDonald's sign. Every time I saw a light of any kind, I exclaimed "light" all the way home.

Years later, as a poet, I have written many poems and made artwork that include varying versions of the phrase *keep looking where the light pours in.*

KEEP LOOKING WHERE
THE LIGHT POURS IN

I've received many questions about this line and where it came from and why I write it so much. It wasn't until I remembered my parents telling me this story that I pieced it together: looking for light started out in a literal way for me.

Now, I don't point out illuminated fast-food signs and shout "light!" like I used to, but I still notice them. I still notice the streetlights that line the sidewalks and how some are bright orange and others bend white. I always notice the one light that flickers in the parking deck and the taillight with the cracked red shell that beams brighter than the others. I notice the moon when it's orange-red and when it's hardly visible and you have to scan the sky to find it. If I step outside at night, I look up immediately to play connect-the-dots with the stars.

In many ways, I haven't changed a lot since I was a child. I'm glad this way of noticing light has stayed with me. Even as I pen these words, outside my window to the right, the sun is rising. As I write, I also keep glancing over, wondering what colors the sunrise will bring today. The past few days it's been a perfect, vibrant pinkish-orange. So far there's a hint of yellow, and it looks like the hues will be subtler today.

Every day I notice light and all its nuances.

But I feel like I notice just as many shadows. I look out the window at this sunrise, but I also see the trees that block my view and keep me from seeing the full range of the sun's glory. I see a metal power line beam towering high above the trees. It's roped with a dozen black cords stretched to the furthest point of tension in both directions. So, yes, there's the sunrise, but there's also all these other obstructions.

Perhaps you've had experiences like this too.

You were trying to have a quiet evening . . . while your upstairs neighbor decided to rearrange their living room.

Your one day off was filled with unexpected phone calls.

You spent time with people you love, but you kept thinking about who wasn't there.

You were enjoying a glorious sunset, but it came on the heels of a tough day.

You remembered the smallest details about the conversation that night under the moonlight: the way he laughed, the way he listened to your stories. And you also remembered how that was the last time you saw each other.

The reason why you remember both sides of these experiences is because all your life you have been learning to paint with both shadows and light. You have been learning how to find the gold amid the dust, even in uncertainty. You crank up the music that takes you back to summer 2003, even though life wasn't perfect back then. You look at pictures of old friends and smile, even though you don't see each other anymore. You've learned how to appreciate both the shooting stars and the flashing lights on the bottom of an airplane, soaring high in the sky in the dead of night. You've learned how to hold it all and be all right.

Not perfect, but all right.

You've been practicing peace your whole life.

You've been taking notice of the good, the bad, and everything in between.

How to feel it all and still breathe.

Yes, there are moments when it seems like too much, and you wish you could get rid of what seems to obstruct your view of the sunrise. But at the same time, all along, you have learned to see the need for the trees. You have learned that even though they keep you from seeing all the beauty of the horizon, they provide oxygen so the earth can breathe. Each tree has a purpose, even when the shadows block the full range of dawn's light.

So if practicing peace feels like a daunting task, as you try to make sense of a world woven with uncertainty, just remember, you're already years into this journey. You've already lived through thousands of sunrises and sunsets. Now is the time to go deeper and learn to see the value in it all.

PRACTICE PEACE BY LEARNING TO SEE VALUE IN IT ALL

As a self-taught visual artist, I've learned a lot about art from the internet. One topic that shows up in a lot of beginner courses and YouTube videos is the "elements of art." This usually refers to the most common features an artist uses to convey their message through their art. One of these features is "value." Value in art has to do with light and the way it creates a variety of shades from black to white. When an artist pays attention to value, they are able to highlight the contrast of their subject in a dynamic way that draws the eye inward to the subject.

Learning how to make use of shadow and light can make all the difference in how we perceive an image. Black-and-white photography is a great example of this. We don't even have to see a scene in full color for our minds to make sense of where the shadows and light are, and as a result, we are able to understand what's happening in the image.

What I love about this concept is that the artist doesn't ignore the shadows. They work with them. The photographer doesn't completely avoid the trees. Instead, they work their subject through the shadows and into the light. They notice where the light pours in through the leaves. Then they play with the shadows of the leaves beneath their feet. Whether a painter, photographer, or filmmaker, they work with light to capture the image, but they don't avoid the shadowy corners.

When it comes to practicing peace, we may want to avoid the shadows. We long for the light-woven moments, and it's sometimes hard to see the value in the darker ones.

If only we could see the sunset without that big tree in the way.

If only we could have a nice Saturday afternoon without anyone interrupting.

If only we could have world peace and a healthy planet without having to talk about politics.

When I look at some of my favorite works of art, I find that they contain more than blues, golds, and greens. There are shadowy colors too. In Alma Thomas's *Starry Night and the Astronauts*, I see the royal blues and dash of warm colors right away. But the longer I look at this piece, the more I see darker blues that are nearly black. My eyes don't gravitate to them immediately, but they are just as much a part of the piece. When I look at Faith Ringgold's *Tar Beach 2*, I see a vibrantly colored quilt that tells the story of the hopes and dreams of a young African American girl named Cassie Louise Lightfoot. Cassie's story is based on Ringgold's own childhood memories of growing up in Harlem, New York. The part of the quilt that catches my eye most is the young Cassie flying in her nightgown through the night sky among the stars. It's there in the shadowy darkness that it seems that Cassie could overcome anything. And the longer I look, the more shadowy colors I see: the brown-black branches stitched to hold up the plants that surround them, the black outline of the George Washington Bridge beyond them, her father's black suspenders and work shoes. Every part of the quilt tells a story.

To paint the shadowy colors, the artist must practice. They don't simply throw random colors together and hope for the best. They learn to look for value in every shade. I have learned a lot from studying shadows and light in art. I have decided that mixing a range of colors and using them to tell a story is a worthy practice, even if it takes a lifetime.

Instead of looking for light only as a way to avoid the shadows, what if we were willing to accept the whole picture? What if we deliberately spent time with those colors that don't scream "joy" like yellow or "love" like red? What if practicing peace is slowing down and realizing there's more to see?

This doesn't mean we can't look where the sunlight pours in. This doesn't mean we can't paint with bold colors or long for the day that we are able to watch a sunrise without power lines in the way. It just means that perhaps we can still breathe deep and make the most of where we are, even if it doesn't look exactly how we hoped or planned.

We don't have to understand everything before we hold both shadow and light.

We don't have to eliminate every unknown before we take action.

We don't have to get rid of the darkness to see where the stars shine through.

PRACTICE PEACE BY EMBRACING THE FULLNESS OF REALITY

I have become curious about some of the feelings that rise up within me when visiting the doctor's office. Recently, when the receptionist handed me the twelve-page packet of new-patient forms, the first thing I wanted to do was rush through, checking off all the preexisting conditions I don't have.

I wish this weren't true, but I felt ashamed for not being able to check "no" for every box. I feel the heavy shadow of having seen both my mother and my sister misdiagnosed and struggle to receive proper treatment for their conditions. As a child, I witnessed my sister's misdiagnosis land her in the hospital. As a result, I fear getting sick. I fear needing help.

What if I'm misunderstood or there's a miscommunication?

What if something is truly wrong and it gets missed?

What if they see trying to figure out my issues as an inconvenience?

What if they walk away feeling like they've wasted their time?

My heart beats faster even as I consider these questions.

Not only do I fear something being wrong, I fear how I might be perceived. When I am not 100 percent okay, it's a fight within me to speak out about how I feel. I want to seem strong and healthy even when I'm not. Even when the doctor is patient and understanding, my fear of being incapable hangs out in the room with me. Shame beams down through the fluorescent lights. I struggle to speak up. I have a hard time feeling that the reality of my pain is valid.

And I know I'm not the only one.

There are many books and articles about the rise of victimhood, and their message is so strong that many actual victims feel like they are to blame for their own trauma. People who are in pain don't feel safe to speak about what they're going through. I didn't realize how often this occurs until I started to write poetry inspired by people's stories.

Since 2017 I have invited people to share their own personal stories with me, and I write poetry and make art as a response.

There are no "rules" for story submissions, and they vary widely in length and subject matter. I never reveal any details about the stories, but I will tell you a few phrases that my responses often include:

> There's no need to apologize for that.
> There is absolutely no excuse for what happened.
> No, you're not bothering me at all by sharing this.

Often when I am reading stories sent to me, I shake my head in anger for the people who were made to question the validity of their experiences. People who are strong in ways they do not know. People who define what it means to survive. I write poetry with the hope of creating space for the words they didn't feel they had permission to say. I write not because I have answers but because I want to be one person along the journey who reminds them that the shadows they have found on the path are real. And so is the morning sun. And they are not alone in facing any of this.

But realizing that *I* am not alone has been hard work. When I sit waiting for the doctor to knock on the door to enter the room for my appointment, I take a deep breath and remind myself that the compassionate words I speak to others are true for me too. I am reminded of these words by therapist Aundi Kolber in her book *Try Softer*: "Suffering is not isolated. It's common to all humanity. . . . When we recognize that we are not unique in our experiencing of suffering, we are more likely to see ourselves as worthy of compassion. We are also less likely to feel as if we are alone; instead, we feel more connected with the human experience."[1]

As I work to change my way of thinking, at the core, I am grateful that I have noticed the need to change. For even though my voice shakes when I tell the doctor something doesn't feel right, I am still breathing through it. I feel anxious, and at the same time, I am breathing through it. I am embracing the reality of something I need to unlearn. It's messy. I'm not fearless right now. But I am breathing through these shadows that tell me to hide what I'm feeling because I don't know what the response will be. And I am learning what practicing peace is for me and what it is not.

Practicing Peace Is Not:

"Everything's okay! I promise!"

"I'll be fine. Don't worry about me."

"I just want everyone to be happy."

"I won't mention what bothered me . . . I'm just trying to keep the peace."

"I'll just stay out of politics."

Practicing Peace Is:

"It's hard to say this, but I'm not okay."

"It's not easy for me to ask, but I do need help."

"I can no longer live to please everyone."

"I will courageously pursue a safe space to speak directly about what I'm feeling right now."

"I am equipped to have hard conversations, knowing even those moments are wrapped in grace. When I choose to be present, there is room for learning, growth, healing, and restorative justice."

Practicing peace is the willingness to go beyond initial reactions and get down to the ones that remind us that, amid our fears, the river still flows. Practicing peace is realizing that even when we struggle to open up, bringing those honest feelings and thoughts into the light matters. There's a whole range of emotions between "everything's fine" and "everything's terrible."

Years ago I was feeling exhausted in the middle of doing work that I loved to do. Even though I had signed my first major contract for a collaboration and I was preparing for the second one, I was questioning my worth. I began to wonder if I was heading down a path that I wasn't equipped to handle. But I wasn't sharing this doubt with anyone. "Who am I to complain when I have so much to be grateful for?" I told myself again and again. At first I felt like I could fight my way through these feelings with positivity and they would go away.

And then one day I left a comment on a social media post of a public speaker that I didn't know very well. She posted a photo of a beautiful restaurant she had been invited to, but she didn't know where the place was, and she "wondered" where it might be. Excitedly, I left a comment tagging the place because I knew where it was and I too wanted to go someday. But I had missed the social cue that this was a rhetorical question. She deleted my comment and proceeded to do another post about how she deleted a comment because "someone" had ruined her surprise. My heart sank in my chest. I felt terrible. I apologized, she responded with a heart emoji, and it was never mentioned again.

However, that little moment was a tipping point. "See, this is why I shouldn't be doing any of this," I told myself. My mind flashed back to moments in high school when my sister and I were singing Johnny Cash songs on YouTube, and we would receive derogatory comments about how we, Black girls, had no business singing these songs. Since then, the possibility of very-real-time reactions that quickly go wrong and the general anxiety that sometimes comes with sharing anything online would sneak up on me.

I had tucked those old days into the dark corners of my mind, and yet here I was, feeling like I was in high school all over again. I was starting to feel anxiety in my body. Suddenly, I was tensing up at the sound of an email notification. I had sweaty palms as I opened social networking apps. I had been called out for my own mistake, and even though it was technically over, it made me physically sick to my stomach. And yet I told no one. I said nothing. I told myself this was my issue to deal with, and it wasn't that big of a deal. But when it got to the point that I couldn't think clearly and calmly while working, I knew it was time to ask for help.

My therapist was the first one I spoke to about any of this. As I told her my story, she looked at me and right away let me know she could see in my posture alone that I was used to having to try to be the strong one and struggled to express my needs. It was time to begin the slow and gentle work out of that way of living. She handed me two lists from the Center for Nonviolent Communication. The first list is a "needs inventory." This list is not exhaustive, but it serves as a starting place for naming our actual needs. Here are a few examples from this list.[2]

We May Need:

acceptance, community, consistency, empathy, space, to understand and to be understood

The second list is the "feelings inventory." It is broken down into two sections. Here are a few examples from this list.[3]

Feelings When Your Needs Are Satisfied:

calm, eager, encouraged, revived, safe, satisfied, secure

FEELINGS WHEN YOUR NEEDS ARE NOT SATISFIED:
anxious, disappointed, discouraged, heartbroken, insecure,
lonely, numb, regretful, worn out, worried

I still refer to these lists regularly. Often my needs and feelings seem too overwhelming, and instead of trying to name them, I distract myself by scrolling through social media or watching television. But when I dare to push into the moment and at least try to name the feeling I'm experiencing, I begin to see that even if I don't know what to do with that emotion at first, there is room for it. And I'm allowed to breathe through it.

One thing I find interesting about the feelings inventory is that the list of feelings when your needs are not satisfied is longer than the one when they are. When I first saw this, I thought, "Well that's a little sad, isn't it?" But the more time I spend with this list, the more I wonder if the "not satisfied" list is longer because these are the feelings people have spent more time with, trying to name them so they can work with them . . . and there's nothing wrong with that because that's how we learn and grow.

PRACTICE PEACE BY GETTING SPECIFIC

There is power in getting specific. It doesn't isolate us. It connects us. Philosophers have had quite a bit to say about how the universals lie in the particulars, but I like how novelist James Joyce put it: "For myself, I always write about Dublin, because if I can get to the heart of Dublin I can get to the heart of all the cities of the world. In the particular is contained the universal."[4] Joyce was the author of a 730-page novel that I once checked out from the library when I was thirteen because I thought it would make me look smarter (full disclosure: I don't think I made it past the first chapter). I believe there's an important lesson about life here. If it's peace we're looking for, getting into the gritty details of our feelings and life experiences is where we should start.

The meaning I gather from Joyce's words is that no two cities are the same, but beneath it all, in every city, there is humanity. We have shared experiences and stories that connect us more than they separate us. But we can't get to those deeper layers without going through the top ones. Before we hop on a plane to go write about a city we've never been to, we can push into the layers of the street we live on. The place we call home. The body we live in every day.

This doesn't mean we don't travel the world or seek out new experiences. But when we're struggling to be present right where we are, we have to ask ourselves, What am I avoiding? Why is it so hard to be right here?

I prefer to say to the doctor, "I'm fine," when the reality is, I'm not. I have needs that must be addressed, experiences I haven't processed, and feelings that are worthy of language. And even though I feel exposed and vulnerable under the harshness of the fluorescent lights, and even when I feel like the trees obstruct my view of the sunrise, when I slow down, I find that no matter the shadows that find me, the sun still shines bold and bright. The ground is still steady beneath my feet. Right here, in this moment, I can name my experiences. I can give language to my feelings, my needs. I see both the lights and shadows in this room. I breathe.

Practicing peace is realizing over and over, as Joyce did, that we are free to push into the particulars. And we don't have to be afraid of them. The details provide valuable insight into who we are, what we do, and the stories that connect us.

Decades ago Tracy Chapman released a song that *Rolling Stone* listed as No. 167 on the list of the 500 Greatest Songs of All Time. It is the highest-ranking song performed and solely written by a female artist on this list.[5] The widely popular song, which you have likely heard, is called "Fast Car."

When Chapman sings about working at a convenience store, a father who is weary from work, and a mother who left to pursue her own dreams, I feel the emotion of it, even though that's not my story. The gritty realism of a "checkout girl" singing about life beyond living in the shelter and the feeling of belonging is a story that was meant to be heard and is deeply felt by people around the world.

What I love about music, literature, and art is that through them we see that there is space for what we are feeling. In her book *The Mystical Now*, British nun and art historian Sister Wendy Beckett says, "Art accepts all the sadness, and transforms it, implicitly affirming that Beauty is essentially the presence of God."[6]

Peace does not mean everything is perfect. Rather, peace means you are able to find your breath, to stay connected to your very life, in the face of gritty realism. You are allowed to express your longing. Your needs. The shadows that linger in the room. You are free to say, "Wait . . . this doesn't sit right with me," even if you don't know what the solution will be. You're allowed to acknowledge that you're experiencing discomfort, even if you struggle to find the right words for it. You're permitted to call attention to what puts others in vulnerable positions, even as you actively work to become educated on the best ways to help.

Be present to whatever you're dealing with right now, knowing that peace is powerful. Endless, and boundless, it is a mighty river in the desert. And you are allowed to arrive with a clenched fist or a heavy mind. You are permitted to enter with a broken heart. You are free to cry out under the cool blanket of the night sky or sit silently and let the piano ballad tremble the words you can't say. You are free to feel abandoned. Free to grieve. Free to embrace the full reality of the pain and suffering within, and in this world. You are free to do these things knowing that even here, the river water still flows. And whenever you're ready, you can seek peace simply by inhaling and exhaling until the last breath you breathe on earth.

In those tender moments, merely breathing might not feel like it's enough. Breathing doesn't take away the grief or sorrow. It doesn't end the conflict. It doesn't make every problem go away. But breathing does give us permission to let it all out, even if tears roll down our cheeks as the exhale leaves our lips.

Growing up, I learned the Bible verse that merely says, "Jesus wept" (John 11:35). It seemed to come up only at camp when there was a Bible-memory-verse game going on. When campers had to pick a verse to memorize, an adult volunteer would inevitably shout out, "Any verse but 'Jesus wept'!" Funny enough, I feel like that verse is one of the most telling of them all. We live in a time when people are seen as weak for crying. Not shedding a tear has somehow become a sign of strength. And yet tears have a holy place.

Your gritty feelings belong. Name them. Embrace the tomb of shadows and sorrows for what they are.

Even here, a new day is coming.

Practice Peace by Looking for Light

I wonder if it's sometimes hard to allow ourselves to drop to our knees under the weight of what we're going through because we feel like if we fall, we might never stop falling. We might never reach the end of our sorrow. So instead, we ignore the shadows because we fear they might consume us. We forget the power of light.

People who notice the stars in the sky or take an extra moment for the sunrise haven't known only joy in their lives. They usually have experienced the cold, black-blue waters of struggle and the long quiet hours of sorrow. Their circumstances have taught them how to just sit and let things be because in the waking hours of grief and despair, sometimes that's all you can do. And the longer they sat there, the more they noticed everything that went unnoticed when all seemed right. They learned not to take things for granted. They learned to treasure where they saw the light.

May we learn to be less afraid of the shadows. And may we realize that just because they are a part of the picture, that doesn't mean that's all there is. We can name them. We can push into the dark and trust that we will be able to breathe deep there. We can openly and honestly talk about what we've been through. And breathe through it. We can speak up about our fears. And breathe through them.

May we also look for the light. We can embrace reality and still find a sense of comfort in "city lights that lay out before us," as Tracy Chapman says. We can still exclaim, "Light! Light! Light!" all the way home under a beautiful, bold, black sky.

In learning to hold both shadow and light, I have been able to practice peace in my daily life. In the following chapters, I will guide you through the rhythms that have gracefully brought me back to the present moment, over and over again—rhythms that have kept me breathing and helped me practice peace.

CHAPTER 4

RHYTHM

If I am ever on a high horse and need to be humbled, I hope someone who loves me takes me to a wedding reception where I will be forced to do the Electric Slide. To the terribly uncoordinated (such as myself), nothing is more humbling than the Electric Slide. Throughout my life, some kind, patient souls have tried to teach me the eighteen steps. Inevitably, I get the first few steps right, but then, when it's time to switch to the other side and repeat those steps, I've forgotten them because now we're facing a different direction. With everyone doing these steps in sync, I mess up, stepping on someone's toes (literally). And that's my cue to exit the dance floor once again.

After years of trying to participate in this communal dance, I think I've finally given up. After all, going to any kind of event with loud music and dancing is an adventure all its own, and I've realized I'm at peace with being a wallflower most of the time.

What's fascinating about being a wallflower is that you're still a part of the pulse of the room. You don't have to be on the dance floor to tap your foot or enjoy the music. You don't have to know the dance moves to feel the celebratory energy rising to the ceiling. Sure, it's a different experience, but you're still a part of the greater celebration taking place.

We learn from music that rhythm isn't only about doing the same thing over and over. Rhythm is about the interrelationship between two kinds of beats, coming together to make the recurring motion.

I've been playing guitar since I was fourteen, and I quickly learned that I like to play rhythm guitar parts much more than the lead guitar parts. While the lead guitarist usually plays the dynamic, recognizable solos, the rhythm guitarist assumes the role of keeping the pulse of the song and gets to play around with the beat. I didn't quite know all the terminology back then, and there's still a lot I don't know, but something intuitive would rise up within me. I knew, as a I strummed along, there was room for the accented, strong beats and also the unaccented, weak beats. And *weak* wasn't a bad word. One song could contain both the thicker sound of the notes and also the softer, quieter ones. And with those parts working together, the rhythm of the song was made.

Rhythms aren't about making everything in our lives the same but about recognizing the interrelationship of different elements coming together to make the songs of our lives. We can't find a rhythm unless we're willing to make room for both the faster and the slower aspects of life. Unless we're willing to see that some parts of the day are for stillness and listening and others for giving and sowing, we won't find a rhythm. In one second, we're inhaling. The next, we're exhaling.

We have to trust that the timing of everything will come together in the way it's meant to. Trusting is important because it means we accept that we don't need to have our daily rhythms figured out every second of the day to be present to them. For instance, you don't have to be a musician to move to the rhythm of the drum. You don't have to be an expert in literature for your heart to sync with the rhythm of a poem. And you don't have to be a conservation scientist to enjoy the many rhythms of nature.

We don't have to be experts to practice creating rhythms in our daily life. We don't have to know the routine in order to dance, sing, or breathe as a way into peace.

There's the Electric Slide, and there's also tapping your feet over in the corner.

There's the well-planned to-do list and ten-year plan, and there's also the day by day, when we inhale, exhale, and find peace in doing what we can.

There's the rushed pace of the concrete, human-made world around us, and then there's also the natural world that invites us to be still.

There are rhythms all around us waiting for us each day. And no one approaches rhythms in the same way. There's room for all of us. What matters is that we each know that finding rhythms isn't about everyone doing the same exact things each day, nor is it about trying to manufacture perfect rhythms all on our own. Finding rhythms is about joining in the pulse of what's already happening,

> with our stronger beats and our softer beats,
> our inhales and our exhales,
> through shadow and Light,
> we experience life,
> every day,
> all by grace.

MUSIC AND PEACE

Recorded music has become a multibillion-dollar industry. We have more music than ever before. As a result, it's easy to forget that music is a sacred form of expression. And through that expression, we take part in something greater than us. Poet John O'Donohue once said, "Music does not touch merely the mind and the senses; it engages that ancient and primal presence we call soul."[1]

When I was growing up, my mother told me the story of Czech composer Antonín Dvořák, who came to the United States in 1892. The National Conservatory of Music of America hired him to help American composers find their voices separate from the more well-known European influences. At the time of his arrival, American concert music sounded more like its European influences, such as Bach, Mozart, and Beethoven. In coming to the United States, Dvořák heard Negro spirituals for the first time. Upon hearing this music, he had a revelation, as he told the *New York Herald* just before he debuted his "New World" symphony: "'The future of this country must be founded upon what are called the Negro melodies,' he declared. 'This must be the real foundation of any serious and original school of composition to be developed in the United States.'"[2]

Dvořák saw what other composers couldn't see at the time: the music was already there. The composer was heavily criticized for these comments as it was controversial to compare the music of Black people in America to that of famous white composers. But Dvořák persisted and went on to give homage to Black spirituals in his own work.

Taking time to enjoy music is a way we can begin to reclaim those spaces within our souls that remind us that right here, in the middle of it all, we are still whole. We are allowed to take in the music before we understand it. We are allowed to listen in and listen well. We are free to close our eyes to the sound of the violin and move our hips to the beat of the drum. Even those of us who can't dance can nod along and let music do what it does so well: invite us into the fold of something more.

Music is permission and freedom to join in the dance of life, without words, without answers. Even when the music plays over computer speakers and we are decades or even centuries removed from those who composed the song, we are participating, as Barbara A. Holmes notes, in the "wonder of surviving together."[3]

Music became a rhythm that helped me practice peace when I was fourteen. My sister and I were being tested for Wilson's disease because of different symptoms we were both experiencing. If every family has their "big thing" that they deal with, my family's has definitely been health issues. I have watched every member of my immediate family, myself included, walk through the unknowns of a life-altering health crisis.

It takes a great deal of courage to share what I've been through medically, because as anyone who has faced health challenges knows, talking about what you're going through can unfortunately come with people judging you, questioning you, not believing you, trying to fix you, trying to pray it away, or treating you differently. Sometimes those people are well-meaning, but it still hurts. Even as I share this part of my story, I hear the voices in my head of those who might discredit me, but I also hear the sound of my own exhale as I breathe deep and write anyway. I remember all the valleys I've crossed to be here and how this too is a part of how I am learning to practice peace.

This potential diagnosis of Wilson's disease left my teenage self with sweaty palms, headaches, and sleepless nights. Even though the survival rate of Wilson's disease was near 80 percent, the other 20 percent left me feeling uneasy. As we waited for test results, I was desperate for anything that could take my mind off of the impending news. One day during this period, we ended up at my grandparents' house. My grandfather had started collecting instruments from various thrift shops and yard sales and teaching himself to play. One of the instruments he had was an electric guitar.

"Do you want to come in here and see this guitar? I'll show you how to play something!" my grandfather offered.

I agreed and proceeded to the room that was slowly becoming the music room. The only light source came from a window in the corner, which was just enough to see the shape of my grandfather's hand as he showed me the chord. As I clumsily moved my fingers toward the fretboard with my left hand, I got ready to strum with my right. Right before I strummed the chord, I heard what I can describe only as the voice of God clearly say to me, "You're going to use this."

My grandfather let me take his guitar home, and I sat with it for some time, trying to teach myself to tune it and play it. There were only a few websites at the time that offered free guitar resources, so I was left to try and piece together a lot of the process myself. I knew very little about playing guitar, but I started practicing the chords I could figure out. I strummed loudly on the electric guitar's strings, even though I didn't have an amplifier. I busied myself with learning whatever I could, though I didn't really know why. I didn't have a plan for how I would use it. I had just heard a song sung to me from the distance that someday I would.

A few weeks later, the test results came back negative for Wilson's disease. Even though my sister and I would both go on to face other health challenges, in that moment we sighed with relief. And now I was starting to make music with the guitar that had found me in the waiting. My grandfather brought a drum set over, and my sister taught herself to play. We ended up finding an amplifier somewhere, I learned a couple of chords, my sister learned a few beats, and we started to play music that would end up changing our lives.

When I was growing up, my mom would play Dvořák's "Going Home" for my sister and me. Years after learning about Dvořák's time in America, I sometimes think about what it might have been like for him to hear Negro spirituals for the first time. And more often than that, I think about what it would have been like for these songs to be sung for the first time. I think about the names I will never know, breathing songs into the open air, humming the tunes of heaven, of Home.

As I clumsily played guitar chords for the first time, feeling simultaneously electrified and calmed by the sound, I felt connected to something ancient, a wisdom much older than me, a way of believing in God and having peace beyond understanding that I will never know in the way my enslaved ancestors did. And at the same time, though my day-to-day life is different from theirs, when I play music, I feel connected to whatever it was that helped them to sing. And that is why I practice music. I practice by playing it, listening to it, and letting it fill the spaces of my home.

Because of the sensory-overload challenges I face, I am usually content with music at a much lower decibel than perhaps what someone else would like. But I have learned to appreciate it that way, for at the lower volume, it becomes a hum in the room, low but filled with vitality, story, rhythm.

In each of our histories, certain songs carry special meanings and stories that are worth making space for in our daily lives. Whether it's a song passed down through your family or a song you used to sing along to on the radio when you were in middle school, the moments when you sing along are moments when you are breathing in and breathing out with the rhythm of the music. As you tap your fingers along the dashboard waiting for the chorus, you take in the lower energy of the verse as it builds to the prechorus. And then you belt out the part everyone knows, the part that gets stuck in our heads. You join in with the vocalist, the bassist, keys player, guitar player, and drummer keeping the chorus moving along. The background vocalists support the melody—as do you and all the other voices who feel the emotion of that song and have learned the lyrics just like you did.

A few times I've had the enormous privilege of playing a song I wrote for a group of people who sang it back to me. I could barely get through the song without thinking about how, in that moment, that song wasn't mine anymore. The song came out of my mouth, but it was up in the air for anyone else to grab and make it their own. And if they wanted to inhale it and breathe it out with me, they could.

It's hard to explain, but when I hear a new song and it speaks to me, I often feel as though the song itself is calling out to me. I can feel it traveling through the air, finding its way to my ear, a gift from the song's creator, who dared to put that feeling to a melody.

The next time you hear a song that speaks to you, I hope you can receive it for the gift that it is. When you feel the bass of the tune that pulled you through that rough day or the rhythm of the ballad that helped you sleep that one night, breathe it in and breathe it out. Inhale on intros and outros, and exhale the parts where you know the words. Hum the tune however you want to. Even if you feel you're the worst singer the world has ever known.

When you dig into the histories of the great songs of the past few centuries, you will find that many of them were made in the in-betweens, for the in-betweens. Somebody had to go through something for that beautiful song to be what it is.

The next time you hear a song that moves you, think about what time it was made in. Look up the year it was written or released. What was happening? What war was tearing through a part of the world? What crisis was their community facing? What tragedy or loss were people inhaling at that time? You don't have to know the personal story of the writer or singer to look at the state of the world and recognize all that the average human being was taking in at that time.

And then pay attention to parts of the song that seem to push forth. Notice the sections that may almost feel like a battle cry, a declaration, or a whisper that barely escaped their lips. Even if the song is instrumental, the violin breathes out an emotion in a different way than a harp would, which is different than what a percussion instrument would convey. Perhaps, amid all that the artist was inhaling at the time, this song was, in one way or another, an exhale. Finally breathing out after taking in so much.

What I am talking about here is using music as a way of reminding us to breathe. To take in what's going on around us, but not to stay there. To recognize our need to exhale. To realize that in the wild of the chaos, we don't have to hold everything in. Even if we can't find the right words, even if we don't have the answers, we can fill the room with music—a small act of rebellion against the dissonance that often pulls us away from peace.

Dissonance, in musical terms, is "a mingling of sounds that strike the ear harshly."[4] The dissonance we hear in daily life might sound like the patterns of our own thoughts when we feel overworked while also feeling like we're not doing enough. Or the way that social media notifications clash with our need for slowness. After too many moments of trying to make sense of the dissonance, music—literal music—can be a reminder that melody, harmony, and rhythm are still possible. As our hearts beat, the drum in the song beats too. We can still know peace, right here.

Approaching Music in a Mindful Way Can Help Us . . .

Slow Down and Feel More Deeply

I close my eyes when I sing so I can feel the song better.

—Mahalia Jackson

Whether you're playing or listening to music, if you want a song to sound as it was intended, you can't rush it. If you listen to a song on double speed, it won't have the same effect. In a fast-paced world, music prompts us to slow down. It reminds us of the unhurried inhales we must take even when we feel pressured to rush our way through. We should let the song find us at the tempo it was meant to and then pace ourselves along with it, inhaling and exhaling where the music pulls back and then lets go, and where the vocalist does the same. How do the words feel in our ears? What wisdom awaits us when we take in music slowly? How might we exhale differently?

Take Deeper Breaths More Often

Stress and anxiety can keep us from taking deeper breaths, and research has shown that music does affect our mood. In an article for Berkeley's Greater Good Science Center, psychologist Jill Suttie presented research on how music affects our health: "Neuroscientists have discovered that listening to music heightens positive emotion through the reward centers of our brain, stimulating hits of dopamine that can make us feel good, or even elated. Listening to music also lights up other areas of the brain—in fact, almost no brain center is left untouched—suggesting more widespread effects and potential uses for music."[5] The research around the effects of music is promising, showing that this timeless art form can have an impact on our lives. We may already know about the effects certain songs have on us, but sometimes in times of stress, we forget the good music could do, especially when we have so many options in our modern times to just check out and grow numb. Practicing peace is a lifelong process of coming back to the present moment over and over again. And when we are overwhelmed with unknowns, or sinking under the weight of stress, we need to do whatever we can to be present with every breath, inhale to exhale, verse to chorus, song to song.

Remember What Is Good

Music is our witness, and our ally. The "beat" is the confession which recognizes, changes, and conquers time.

—JAMES BALDWIN

In the documentary *Alive Inside*, social worker Dan Cohen brings music to dementia patients in a nursing home. He asked the family members of the residents to provide him with the residents' favorite songs, and he plays those songs for them. "Some people, who had seemed unable to speak, proceed to sing and dance to the music, and others are able to recount when and where they had listened to that music."[6] A lot of research is still being done on music's effect on our memory and also how it affects the process of making new memories.[7] One thing for sure is that the positive emotions we experience with the songs we love are not to be overlooked. Even when we feel that our hands are tied and there is nothing we can do to change our circumstances, we can still bring music into the atmosphere. We can turn on the songs from our childhood or adolescent years that made us feel like we had a little bit more room to breathe. We can turn it on, sit, listen, and do nothing else. It is easy to forget what a gift it is to have the ability to listen to recorded music or simply feel its vibrations as it fills the room. Make room for good music. Make room to remember what is good.

Remember That We Are a Part of Something Greater Than Ourselves

> *I don't know the answers to anything. I just come to sing you these songs that have been inspired by something that I hope is deeper and bigger than myself.*
>
> —Leonard Cohen

Leonard Cohen spoke these words at a performance of his many years ago.[8] He was preparing to sing his well-known "Hallelujah," and for me, these words affirmed what already felt true about the song. While the song tells one story, at the same time it speaks to the inner wrestlings and exhaled hallelujahs that millions of people have known in their own lives. When people sing together, they are inhaling and exhaling together. And in that collective song, all the voices rising and falling together point to something larger than ourselves. Whenever you hear or see people singing together, consider this: it isn't often that we are joined together in this manner, taking inhales and exhales in the same rhythm and time. Every person singing has a different story and experiences that led to that very moment, and yet at that point, there's one story, a larger story. Breathe it in and breathe it out, together.

Seek Out the Music of Everyday Life

Music has a breadth far beyond simply listening to recorded music. Music is woven into everyday life. Consider the songs of the birds, who have been faithfully humming their tunes every day, even long before recorded music came along. Consider the rhythmic sound of footsteps climbing a wooden staircase. Think of the hum of an automobile's tires rotating on the pavement. While teaching students how to make percussion sounds using pots, pans, and other household objects, percussionist Sheila E. said, "I feel that I can take anything and make it music."[9] She went on to show how one could go about listening and looking for music in daily life and how she has incorporated these everyday sounds into her own music. When we see children turn containers into drums or brooms into guitars, we are reminded that we don't have to be professional musicians to look for the music in the day-to-day.

One thing that can keep us from noticing the musical rhythms of daily life is that often our days are based on goals and what we achieve. But music is not about a goal. Music is an experience we enter into. The only product at the end of it is that you were present to it. Oh, what a difference it would make if we could be present to our days in the same way. What if we could end each day exhaling with a sense of peace, saying, "I engaged. I listened. I was present." And what if that was enough?

THE PRACTICE

THE HISTORY

Listen to "Going Home" from "Largo" of Symphony no. 9 in E Minor, Op. 95, "From the New World," performed by Kathleen Battle, written by Antonín Dvořák and William Arms Fisher. This version of "Going Home" highlights different instrumentation and Battle's voice in a way that calls to remembrance the history of the piece and also the legacy it leaves. Listen to this piece while reflecting on the many possible narratives woven in and out of the story.

WHOLENESS

CHAPTER 5

WHOLENESS

At age sixteen, I started my first job at PacSun at Mall at Stonecrest in Lithonia, Georgia. My favorite part of the job was to fold and stack shirts around the store. One day a family came in, shopping as usual, and when I went over to help them, the dad said to me, "Hey, check this out! I managed to put these shirts back in the right order!" I could tell that he was mostly making conversation, but as I looked at the shirts he had looked at and then put back, I genuinely thought he did a good job, to which I exclaimed, "Congratulations! You did a good job."

Immediately, the dad's face turned sour, and the family walked away.

I thought about this moment for a long time. What had gone wrong?

I was a teenager at the time, and I wasn't aware that my natural speaking voice is rather monotone. And of course I didn't know yet that as a result of being autistic, my inability to naturally speak with a great degree of inflection and nuance can at times make me come across as rude or cold. When I congratulated the dad, I meant it. I took my job seriously and spent a long time learning to fold the shirts neatly. I can honestly say it was the highlight of my work day. And it was cool to see a customer get it right on a whim. But now I see that even though I was genuinely excited, the tone of my "congratulations" likely did not come across in the way I thought it did, and the shopping dad probably thought I was being sarcastic.

When I finally figured this out, I sat with it for a long time. How many times had this happened and I didn't realize it at the time? How many times had I come across as cold when I thought I was speaking as clearly and concisely as possible?

I have spent time thinking about these possible misunderstandings that others may have forgotten long ago. I have feared that I made people feel bad about themselves even though it wasn't my intention. As a result of this fear, I have often felt pressured to use as much inflection in my voice as possible so that I'm not misunderstood. I have put a lot of work into this, and while it's become a part of life that I accept, it's also exhausting.

However, slowly but surely I have found that there's another side to this struggle.

Not long ago I started making audio recordings of my poems. I had not performed much spoken word poetry before, but I was curious about trying to read some of my poems out loud. As I shared them, the feedback I received was incredibly kind. I don't know what I was expecting, but many of the responses surprised me. The comments I received included phrases such as "you have such a calming voice" and "your voice is so peaceful."

I had never thought of my speaking voice in that way. I was convinced my voice needed fixing and changing. I wasn't necessarily trying to speak in a peaceful or calming way. This was how I spoke because I had spent so much time learning when, where, and how to use inflection. How to ease into what I was saying so it didn't come across as too harsh. How to approach certain consonants such as *b* and *p* slowly because those letters tend to hit a bit harder and cause me to raise my volume without realizing it.

I was shocked that all this planning and strategy and striving could be received as "calming," because it certainly didn't come from a calm place.

But as I listen back to recordings of myself, I have slowly begun to appreciate them. I may not be able to hear exactly what others hear, but there is something worth acknowledging and celebrating. My ability to speak calmly and to be mindful of every sound that leaves my lips has allowed me to connect with others in ways I would never have imagined possible.

I can now see that in the same way I found joy in the practice of folding shirts, eventually I learned to find joy in practicing ways to speak.

I want to live in a world where autistic people and others with disabilities feel safe and free to breathe the way they were meant to. Being autistic and also a woman, I have often felt the pressure to speak with a higher pitch than is comfortable or to add inflection to my voice in certain places because of all the expectations around how people think a woman should be in the world. This only gets more complicated as a Black woman, as we have historically been portrayed in the media as stern, mad forces and not much else.

I also want to live in a world where people like me are acknowledged for the hard work they put in to survive in a society that isn't always designed for those who aren't "normal." Without even knowing anything about my autism diagnosis, the people in my community made me feel acknowledged by sharing with me that my voice—the very thing that made me anxious—was calming for them. They helped me see that even while practicing how to use my voice was a struggle, as I read those poems, my words sounded a bit like peace.

The thing about practicing peace is that we don't always feel like we're practicing. In the moment it might feel like survival, just barely making it through, trying to handle what life throws our way. But when we look back, we see that mistakes and misunderstandings don't have to keep us from becoming. We can continue to inhale and exhale despite the awkwardness and confusion. We can continue to breathe as we learn from those moments and move on.

Seeing life this way can take time. It took me over ten years to realize that the shopping dad probably thought I was being sarcastic. In the grand scheme of things, that was a pretty small moment—one that the dad and his family may not even remember. And yet, despite how small it was, I ended up learning not only what I struggle with but also what makes me uniquely *me*.

I find peace in knowing I will continue to learn and grow as I go. I will continue to practice with the small moments, which might end up sounding like peace later.

Even though I may not always be able to see it in real time, the moments when I am practicing peace are truly beautiful. In the moment, practicing may feel like struggle, but later on I see that in the practicing, working through the tension of what my voice was and what I felt it had to be, I was learning to embrace the wholeness of who I am.

Peace is something I am learning to feel in my physical body too. After giving birth to my son, I experienced a lot of new complications. Not only did my body no longer look the same, but I could no longer squat to pick something up or close my legs without feeling pain. From the physical therapist to the chiropractor, and with warm baths in between, I tried everything. But even when there was improvement, my body never looked or felt the same.

When I looked in the mirror, I would exhale in the form of a sigh, and then a question: "Could I have at least one of the two—look the way I did or feel the way I did?"

The issues persisted, and it took a long time before I could squat in a way that felt somewhat normal. I grew impatient with myself as I felt like my recovery time didn't line up with others' experiences that I had read online. It was at that time, for the first time, I was forced to focus on breathing with every move I made while I was at home.

When I am out in the world, I often feel overwhelmed and have to take deep breaths. But at home, I didn't have to focus on my breathing as much because I feel comfortable and free there. But now, with my body acting in ways I didn't understand, every movement felt like a question mark. "Can I do this? Can I move this way?"

The only way through those movements was breathing, mindfully inhaling and exhaling as I performed basic tasks. As I inhaled, my whole body was full with this breath. As I exhaled, I filled the space around me with the exhale. I moved the way I could. I learned to pace myself. I learned to breathe my way through each movement. It felt like a lot of work, but ultimately, it taught me something: there was room for peace within my body. My body that I struggled to understand and make sense of in the postpartum months was finding its way to peace, one move of a limb at a time.

I still hold on to this peace in my body because while I have seen improvement in this particular area, I never got back to feeling or looking the way I did before, and that's okay. I am at peace with knowing that with every inhale and exhale, I am literally breathing life into a new version of my body, learning to accept it and embrace the wholeness of every stage of life.

Embracing Wholeness
Can Help Us . . .

See Ourselves in a Different Way

Only connect! That was her whole sermon. . . .
Live in fragments no longer.

—E. M. Forster

We embrace wholeness by making connections, by realizing that our strengths and weaknesses inform one another. Let us keep connecting to what is beautiful even when we don't feel beautiful ourselves. We may not be sure how to feel about our own stretch marks, but we have learned to admire the stretch marks of the tall oak tree. It may take time and grace for us to see ourselves in the same way, but by seeing the beauty of a God-fingerprinted tree, unafraid to stretch with the years and become who she was meant to be, we are well on our way. We learn to see that the same light that shines on that tree shines on us too. Let us keep connecting to nature. Let us keep admiring what is beautiful around us even when it's hard to see it within ourselves, and in time we will discover that we are worthy of the same grace we extend to the tree. We are not fragmented. We are whole. It takes time to remember, but it's true.

See Our Stories in a Different Way

We're never as far along as we think, because the spiritual
journey is circular. We are always repeating ourselves,
returning to old themes, reexamining the same issue
from a different angle and from the vantage point of a
different season. We don't move on; we return wiser.

—Renita J. Weems

Wholeness

Of course, we could spend all our time thinking about what could have happened differently. Or instead, we can consider what we have learned and how we can carry it with us into the future. Remember that our stories are a cycle, and when we wish we could have done something differently, as long as we're living, it's not too late to circle back, having learned more than we knew before. When we face adversity again, we will face it with new wisdom. We learned from the past. We will know what to do.

Recognize That Our Struggles Can Help Those Who Have Similar Struggles

Deep calls to deep . . .

—Psalm 42:7

In sharing my struggles with learning to accept my voice, I must admit that I winced as I wrote the words. It seemed like such a silly thing to battle with in the larger picture of life. I could hear imagined critical voices telling me it wasn't a big deal. But I held my breath, barely getting the words to the page, and at the end of it, an exhale. Not because I knew how every person would receive my story, but because I knew I had spoken the truth.

Sharing our struggles is difficult because in that moment, we're choosing to go deeper. We choose to let people deeper into our stories, which can make us feel uncomfortable. We may even fear that letting people see our deeper selves might mean that we're opening ourselves to possible pain and rejection. However, when we choose to be vulnerable, we open up opportunities for connection with others who seek to do the same. This affinity doesn't always happen right away, and that's okay. In time, the right person will be grateful that you chose to share. They will be on the receiving end of your learning to embrace the wholeness of your story—even the difficult parts. And when you choose to go deeper by sharing your struggles, you help them to go deeper too.

THE TREE

Find a tree nearby, perhaps in your neighborhood or in the parking lot where you work. Notice what makes this tree special. Is it its height or its age? Is the bark thick? Are the limbs long and thin? Pay attention to all the tree's characteristics. If you don't know what type of tree it is, that's okay. Just simply notice what makes the tree beautiful. Take it in.

FREEDOM

CHAPTER 6

FREEDOM

I have a complicated relationship with salads. Mostly, I avoid them. At restaurants, throughout my life, I've sat across from many people who have ordered a salad, and it never ceases to amaze me how much energy one has to give to dig through the bowl to get all the ingredients on the fork for a good bite. Sunflower seeds and crumbles of cheese slide around the plate as you try to stack half of a gushy tomato on top of a rock-solid crouton on top of the lettuce that's already on the fork, drenched in dressing, holding on for dear life.

After trying multiple salads on multiple menus and even making my own at home, I've pretty much given up on them. I'm also not convinced of the salad fork either, which seems to be designed to help you attack the lettuce more aggressively and bring the other ingredients along with it. It seems to me that we ask a lot of this poor lettuce, to hold its own and hold everything together on a plate where the other ingredients are seeking out their own moment to shine.

I recently asked my husband what he loves about salads, and he proceeded to tell me about how he likes all the combinations he can make. He went on for a few minutes describing what he likes about different sweet and savory pairings and the varying textures one could add to a salad.

Eventually, I interrupted him and asked, "But it doesn't bother you that you have to spend so much time stacking everything up? Isn't it frustrating trying to stack the crouton on top of the tomato on top of the lettuce?"

"No, not at all," he responded. "Because I put the tomato on the fork first, then the lettuce, then the crouton."

Yeah. That's just too much trouble for a lunch break.

But what's fascinating to me about this scenario is that what's too much trouble for me isn't always too much trouble for everyone else. The very thing that stresses me out about the salad is somewhat of a lunchtime adventure for my husband, who enjoys poking around the plate and delighting in all the different combinations.

I look at the salad and think, "This would be so much better if the spinach were cooked and, better yet, over pasta," while others look at it and see a fresh mixture of ingredients to explore. I may never understand the love for salads, but I do understand this: salad is not for me. There are other valid ways of getting the nutrients I need.

I think this approach also applies to the way we take care of ourselves as a way of practicing peace. Many practices out there are healthy and could have an enormous benefit, but they might not work best for us. As I've gotten older, and as I have learned the ways that I am unique, I have discovered the freedom to explore different ways to practice peace. Even though breathing is something we all have in common, there's no one way to breathe. There is also no one way to practice peace.

I once asked my audience, "Where do you go just to take a deep breath?" To no one's surprise, the answers varied widely. For some, it's a room in their house. For others, a moment on the balcony of their apartment. Some go to a park where they can be around others. Others search for wherever they can be alone.

As someone who has to take a lot of deep breaths throughout the day to pace myself, I have noticed that the way we practice peace is also not the same in every season of life. Going back to salads, my parents say I had no issue with them when I was growing up. I also loved ranch dressing, and back in the day, I would "accidentally" pour too much ranch on my salads. Today I can't bear even the smallest drop of ranch. I have no idea what happened, other than maybe I reached my ranch quota early in life. But I do know, what I enjoy has changed over the years. This includes the places I go to seek peace.

When I was a touring musician, I practiced peace in a variety of ways. Back then I didn't know I deal with sensory overload, but after we would play our set, I could hardly think straight and often felt like I could cry, even if I emotionally felt fine. I would dart to the tour bus, where I would lie in my bunk in darkness and stay there for a while. When the show was still going, I'd have rare moments when no one would be on the bus, and I could just sit there and do nothing but breathe.

Another place I practiced peace was in the lobbies of the concert venues. Most of the time when I was playing a show as a solo act, I was one of the opening acts, meaning I was usually finished with my part pretty early on in the event. I noticed that the lobby of the event center or the vestibule of the church was usually mostly empty at this point. I would often end up by the tables where the artists' merch was set up, including my own. It was during this time, before the end of the show, that I'd get to meet other people who were lingering around like I was. I enjoyed meeting people in this way because it wasn't as crowded as it would be once the show ended. I also loved listening to the live music of the other acts, but it was significantly less draining on my senses when I could listen from the lobby. Out here, in the lobby, there was room to breathe. There was room to still be a part of what was going on in a way that I was able to.

In those moments on tour when I was dealing with undiagnosed autism and a sensory processing disorder, I learned the importance of getting creative in seeking out room to breathe in daily life. Being in a healthy community with others is such a beautiful way to practice peace because being with people we feel safe and comfortable around gives us permission to exhale. Sometimes we find community jumping in unison with our one hundred closest friends at the front of the stage, and sometimes we find it lingering in the mostly empty lobby with the other lingerers.

I still remember watching in amazement as certain artists I toured with left the stage exhausted from the performance but also electrified and enlivened from the experience. I watched in disbelief at the artists who flung back on stage for encores and managed to bring up the already high energy of the room to the point that you felt like it could break the ceiling.

I stood sidestage far too many nights, questioning myself, wondering why I lacked the charisma and energy to put on a performance like that. I had spent years perfecting my craft, trying to be the best artist I could be, but when I left the stage, I always felt like I could collapse. I may not have had a name for my struggles back then, and I may have had a hard time loving myself for who I was, but I did manage to find room to breathe. When I would head to the tour bus to have a quiet moment or roam around the lobby away from the noise in the arena, I was finding moments of peace amid the chaos. I was finding that there was still room to inhale, exhale, and be who I was, even when the world felt loud and rushed around me.

Years later, when I started writing poetry for one person at a time, I was fully aware that what I write is informed by those one-on-one interactions with those I met in the lobbies, roaming around, exchanging stories, one city, one person at a time. I still remember many of the conversations that happened in those spaces, and I even ended up meeting a few friends I still keep in touch with. I will always remember to write to the one in the lobby.

Slowly but surely, I have learned other ways to get the nutrients I need. There's more than one way to find healthy moments of connection and community. I must welcome those different ways. I must accept what makes me *me*. There's more than one way to find freedom to breathe.

With Freedom, We . . .

Practice Peace by Deciding We Can Do Things Differently than Others

We spend our younger years learning all the many ways that the world divides itself into groups. We learn everything that is expected of us, and we receive many messages about how we should be in the world. Even something as simple as taking a standardized test in grade school is an indicator for how a child might be successful later in life. From there, many tests we take, on paper and off, are presented as proof for how the future will look for us. But as Mary Oliver so beautifully states in her poem "The World I Live In," the world is "wider than that."[1] There are many ways to grow. There are many ways to get the nutrients we need. The more we can accept the endless diversity of our differences and all the ways we grow, the more we can begin to discover who we are beyond the tests that we pass or fail. The more we will find freedom to embrace our uniqueness.

Here's to recognizing that the way we come alive in this world might not look like everyone else's, and that's okay.

Practice Peace by Naming What We Will Say No To

Your wellness hinges on your boundaries.

—NEDRA GLOVER TAWWAB

In her book *Set Boundaries, Find Peace*, licensed therapist Nedra Glover Tawwab talks about the importance of setting healthy boundaries and being assertive about saying no. She discusses the many story lines that keep us from setting healthy boundaries, including the fears around how our boundaries might negatively affect others.[2] Learning to set boundaries and say no is important work, even when it comes to small opportunities. The more we can learn when and where to say no, the more we will find that these practices give us room to breathe more deeply.

Cleaning out the crowded spaces of our busy lives will take a while, and parting with some of what we held so dear may be hard, but in the end we'll discover we have more room— room to create, dream, live, and breathe.

So here's to saying no when we feel like we should respond to the text right away.

Here's to saying no when we feel like we should say yes to the event just because everyone else is going.

There is grace for us to be here, as we are, and to say no and create boundaries around the things that drain our energy but we feel like we *should* do.

For the sake of our well-being and our physical ability to breathe, let us name the places where we are willing to say no.

Practice Peace by Naming What We Will Say Yes To

bloom how you must

—LUCILLE CLIFTON

Sometimes we hold back on saying yes out of fear. Fear of how we might be perceived. Fear that we might not be successful. Fear that we are unworthy. Something as simple as wanting to say yes to a slower evening with a cup of tea might be overshadowed by the fear that we'll be even further behind if we don't get to our remaining tasks. But here's what remains true: there will always be to-do lists and responsibilities that call our names.

At the same time, we must trust that we are worthy of growth. We are worthy of sunlight and care and everything it takes to bloom the way we were meant to. We can deny care only for so long. We can ignore the ways that we need to be nurtured only for so long. Say yes to opening the window even if it doesn't change everything. It changes something. Say yes to the song that you feel is a little cheesy. It's special to you, and it doesn't matter what others think. Say yes to whatever helps you bloom how you were meant to.

THE PRACTICE

THE PLACE

Notice the places, especially public places, where you feel the most freedom to be yourself. Is it in a corner of a nearby park? A favorite coffee shop filled with other locals? The quiet lobby of an ongoing event? As you move about your day, notice the places where you have the freedom to inhale the moment for what it is and exhale, at peace, knowing that in this space, you are free to just be, as you are, even if only for a little while.

COMMUNITY

CHAPTER 7

COMMUNITY

One of my favorite parts of a nonfiction book is the bibliography. For me, the bibliography is more than a list of every book the author references in their work; it's a paper trail of wisdom that has in one way or another affected the author's message. One day I was spending time in the bibliography of a favorite book and noticed that a few of the authors referenced were authors I had seen reference one another in other works. It was at this moment it occurred to me that these authors were a part of a community. I wasn't sure if these authors were friends in real life or if they had even met before, but suddenly it dawned on me that they were a part of one another's paper trail of wisdom. Each person's work had informed the work of the others. They shared thoughts and ideas even if they never shared a physical space.

Something that has kept me from peace in my life is feeling like I'm not doing community the "right way." As a kid and as an adult, I've struggled with making friends, and I often wonder if I reach out to people often enough or if I'm good at fostering community. Now, of course, if you live in a neighborhood and go to work, school, or church, you are automatically a part of a community in some way. What I'm talking about here is that overlap of "community" and "friends" where within the community you're a part of, you have a smaller group that you're closer to.

I once did a poll on social media asking this question:

Have you ever struggled making friends as a kid or an adult? In response, 60 percent of people said yes, while the other 40 percent said no. While the 60 percent made me feel less alone, I couldn't stop thinking about the 40 percent who said no. I couldn't help but wonder what magical knowledge about making friends they possessed that the rest didn't. What did they know that I don't?

I didn't see any of the faces or names of the 40 percent, but I wondered if these were the groups of friends hanging together that I often look at and wonder, "How did they meet? How are they so close? Have they always been this close?" Were these members of the mom groups and the book clubs and the groups of friends who take trips together?

For some of you reading this, this curiosity may seem rather elementary and simple, and perhaps you're a part of the 40 percent that has never had to ask these kinds of questions. You already have a group of people you consider your community, and you're happy with that. And I am happy for you too because I think a sense of belonging is something everyone desires and deserves. This is exactly why I've chosen to dig deeper into what it means to be a part of a community, especially as an adult.

Merriam-Webster defines *community* as "a unified body of individuals."[1] Cambridge defines it as "the people living in one particular area or people who are considered as a unit because of their common interests, social group, or nationality."[2] These definitions make me realize that the kind of community I tend to focus on most is the kind I see gathering in a physical location. When I think of community, I tend to think of a physical group of people with common interests doing something together. And then I find myself growing anxious for the physical groups of people that I'm not a part of, such as a local moms' group or a monthly gathering of artists. However, what if community was broader than physical location? There are all kinds of reasons as to why one might not have a close physical community: living through a pandemic, moving to a new city, becoming a new parent, graduating from college, and the list goes on and on. And yet, in my own life, I have felt pressure to be much more physically connected with others than I have been able to be. This pressure has caused me to doubt and question myself as I wonder, "Am I doing enough when it comes to making friends? Do we have enough like-minded people we can hang out with as a family? Are we seeing them often enough?"

I recently moved to a new city, and yes, finding community is a process, one that I will continue to work out. In the meantime, I am recognizing that not being in the same physical space with others does not mean I can't have community.

I wonder if the reason why I love bibliographies in the backs of books is because they remind me of the bibliography of my own life. Even though I have lived in over twenty cities in five states and the group of people I see every day has changed drastically over the years, I still carry many of my friends' words with me. I have friendships that have only grown over the years even as the miles between us grew. And even though we don't talk all the time, we can easily pick up where we left off, diving into the deep end of the topics that connect us, without fear.

I have a friend on the other side of the country, Sarah, who sends me the most thoughtful texts and also lets me know it's okay if I can't text back right away. She's told me that she just sends nice things that make her think of me. I have another friend, Rachel, whom I met through blogging years ago. We have never lived in the same place, and yet when we exchange book recommendations and talk about them over the phone, I feel as though we are stopping by each other's porches, swapping books. I had a friend years ago, Deanna, who studied art history. When I went to a museum with her, she opened my eyes to seeing art in a new way.

And then there was a girl who lived on my floor freshman year of college who introduced herself to me at one of the new student events. I asked her about her T-shirt, which featured a song lyric of her favorite band. This band intrigued me, and later that day, she stopped by my room. She had burned a CD for me with her favorite songs from that band as well as some other bands she thought I might like. For whatever reason, I never saw her on campus much after that. We never ended up hanging out, and I think she transferred to a different school the next semester. However, from that CD, I discovered new bands that I still regularly listen to today. I don't even remember the girl's name, but I remember the silver disc on which she wrote all the band names and song titles with ultrafine-point purple and blue permanent markers. I remember every song on that CD. What she gave me that day is a part of my bibliography.

Today the playlists on my phone are more than just playlists. Everyone from the songwriters to the people who told me about the band are a part of the bibliography that made me who I am today.

Whenever I feel lonely and wonder if I'm doing community the right way, I turn to my own bibliography. Over the past few years, I have started filling a journal with nothing but quotes I love. Some of the quotes are lines from poems, song lyrics, and entire paragraphs from favorite authors, but some are also things my friends have said to me. A few are even comments I've overheard from strangers that I found insightful or hilarious. There are even a few individual words in there, such as *Macedonia* because when my dad said it in a sermon once, it sparked something in me to write a song about Macedonia, and I ended up visiting North

Macedonia years later. All these quotes and words are a part of my bibliography. Even in the smallest ways, this journal represents a part of the community I belong to.

I will continue to look for ways to build community in my city, and I will continue to practice being vulnerable and making connections face to face. At the same time, I breathe deep, knowing I am a part of a large community with arms that reach out across the world. I will inhale the wisdom of friends from near and far and exhale knowing that by being in community with them, I have been a part of something more.

RETHINKING COMMUNITY CAN HELP US . . .

Give Ourselves a Break

With so many devices and responsibilities to keep up with in modern life, many of us feel pressured to stay connected all the time. The fear of missing out on the fun or on something important can cause us to feel anxious if we're not able to be present as often as we feel like we should. As we navigate different in-person groups, online groups, family group chats, voicemail boxes, email inboxes, and social media groups, we have to remember that always being available doesn't automatically equate meaningful connections. We can build community slowly over time. We are allowed to say yes to some events and no to others. If your schedule is busy or you're too tired to attend a function, breathe deep and remember that community and relationships are bigger than a one-time event. You have the opportunity to engage in a rhythm of rest— rest that you will need to reenter the world.

Honor Those Who Have Paved the Way

Life is a cycle, but it's not a cycle we travel alone. Whatever part of the life cycle we are stepping into, whether it's a brand-new call to adventure or a season of rebirth and healing, someone has blazed that trail before us. We might not travel with these people physically side by side, but we are a part of the same community. With their books, music, text messages, words of wisdom, and burned CDs of favorite songs, they pave the way for us to carry on. By rethinking the idea of community, we remove the pressure to be always searching for the right group to be a part of, only to feel restless, dissatisfied, or left out when we don't find it right away. By reflecting on those who paved the way, we are already a part of countless overlapping communities that reach out across the world. Understanding this connection, we can seek community in the present moment, knowing we are not as alone as we may feel.

THE PRACTICE

THE BIBLIOGRAPHY

Create your own bibliography. The technical definition of *bibliography* is "a list of the books referred to in a scholarly work,"[3] but it doesn't have to be anything that intense. To create your own personal bibliography, all you need is a blank, sturdy notebook. I recommend a hardcover notebook if you want something that lasts. Over the next week, pay attention to quotes, song lyrics, verses, and phrases that stand out to you. Jot them down on your phone, and write down where you heard or read them. In the evenings, take the quotes and write them in your notebook. Repeat this process as often as you like. Return to the book every so often to read through your notes. Reflect on who said which words and the context of each quote. Keep coming back to it. See something new every time. Learn from your community.

EMPATHY

CHAPTER 8

EMPATHY

Recently I watched a documentary on abstract artist Hilma af Klint. I decided to watch this film after encountering her work online, and I had to know the story behind her art.[1] Something about her work took me someplace else, even just from observing it on my tiny computer screen. I felt seen in these paintings, which was interesting considering these were abstract paintings. As it turns out, I wasn't alone in feeling this way. The documentary revealed that when her work was shown, years after her death, people fell to their knees and cried at the sight of these colorful otherworldly spirals, shapes, and symmetric lines that are painted on canvases that are nearly as tall as the room.

Over the course of my life, art has regularly made me feel seen. Yes, I've had many face-to-face encounters where I have felt seen by people, but it usually takes me weeks, months, or sometimes even years to process the full weight of connections that I've had with others. Something about art reminds me that I don't need permission to be myself. When I am standing before a painting in a museum, I don't need permission to feel. To take up space. To breathe.

To be seen is to be on the receiving end of empathy.

The word *empathy* found its way into our modern lexicon relatively recently. In her book, *You Must Change Your Life*, Rachel

Corbett tells this story. In 1860s Germany, doctor Wilhelm Wundt began foundational work in the field of psychology by studying reaction times "to bridge the gap between voluntary and involuntary attention, between the brain *and* the mind."[2] In the next generation, philosopher Theodor Lipps drew a link between Wundt's work and his own work in aesthetics. This led him to study why art affects us in such profound ways. Lipps ended up finding additional inspiration in one of his student's dissertations, as he spoke of this concept of *Einfühlung*, which literally meant "feeling into." It was a way of describing how people brought their emotions and memories to what they were gazing at. The first known use in English was in 1909, pulling from the Greek word *empatheia* (in pathos).[3]

> Empathy explained why people sometimes describe the experience of "losing themselves" in a powerful work of art. Maybe their ears deafen to the sounds around them, the hair rises on the backs of their necks, or they lose track of the passage of time. . . . When a work of art is effective, it draws the observer out into the world, while the observer draws the work back into his or her body. Empathy was what made red paint run like blood in the veins, or a blue sky fill the lungs with air.[4]

From art and into everyday interactions, *empathy* has become a word we use to describe our desire and need to "feel into" other people's life experiences. Yet entering that deep space is anything but a simple process. It takes time. Energy. It's complicated. To express empathy means entering a story that might challenge your narrative. To express empathy is to do away with questions like the following:

How did they end up in that situation in the first place?
Why can't they just pull themselves up like everyone else?
Why are they struggling so hard with something so simple?

Empathy operates from a different set of questions:

How can I help this person know there is no shame in what
they are experiencing?
Amid all that I don't understand, what's at the heart of the
matter?
How can I support this person today?

There is nothing easy about asking an empathetic question. The discomfort of asking these questions is why it's sometimes easier to avoid them, especially when it comes to asking those we don't agree with. It's easier to avoid the idea of change than it is to address the fear of the future. It's easier to preach moving on than it is to address the wounds of the past. And it's easier (and significantly more profitable) to send a message of us versus them from a platform than it is to get down into the hurt at the heart of an injustice.

We have spent centuries sweeping emotions under the rug. Sometimes that has looked like telling boys that men don't cry or not naming our emotions and seeing them as valid. Through advertisements and political campaigns, we have promoted individual happiness as a destination, as if it's a place we can visit on a cruise. As a result, when we look around, if someone is struggling and not happy, it may feel like it's their fault and it's solely up to the individual to fix every issue in their life. While personal responsibility is incredibly important, we need support and understanding from one another. We need to hold the door for one another, even if we don't technically have to.

The reason I am so passionate about this is because I keep thinking about the years leading up to my autism diagnosis. When I first asked my former doctor for help, I received no empathy. All I received was the message that whatever I was struggling with wasn't that big of a deal and I needed to take it upon myself to figure it out. What gave me the courage to continue seeking help were the women online who shared their experiences with being diagnosed. Suddenly, I realized two things at once: yes, I was struggling to figure out what was going on neurologically, but I didn't have to struggle alone. I didn't have to feel like a failure because I wasn't able to get through this on my own. I needed support. I needed someone who was willing to listen. I needed empathy and I found it, and it made all the difference.

Having been on the receiving end of empathy, I now consider it my duty to pass it on. I am where I am today because of the people who were willing to listen to my story and stories like mine without judgment.

The more I reflect on my own experience, the more I want this freedom and understanding for others. I want to live in a world where more people feel free to open up, to finally stop holding everything in and exhale what they're going through, knowing people will be willing to listen and support them.

We have to open up. We have to exhale. And to do this, we need empathy. We need spaces where people are reminded daily that they are free to feel into the hurt, anger, and grief they've been forced to keep under wraps.

So how do we do this?

Art is one of the most powerful forces we have to foster a sense of empathy.

Through art, in its many forms, we can begin to probe at

the words that are hard to say out loud. And the more we talk and listen to one another, the more opportunities we'll have to lean into those shared emotions. If we're constantly shut off from others, not sure when, where, how, or if we're safe to open up, we'll continue to hold everything in. Anger will go into the underbelly. Resentment will build beneath the layers. Fear will lie and tell us to keep it all inside because no one will understand. Art is a bridge between busy, closed-off souls and empathy. Art demystifies big emotions and illuminates the humanity that exists between us. Art fosters connections we didn't even know we needed. It helps us gain an understanding of stories we didn't even know existed. Art doesn't just say, "I know how you feel." It weaves the message "Come to me, all you who are weary" (Matthew 11:28) into the fabric of our collective being.

According to the Cambridge Dictionary, *art* is "the making of objects, images, music, etc. that are beautiful or that express feelings."[5] When you make things to express your feelings, you are engaging in making art. Even if you haven't played piano in thirty years or have never picked up a paintbrush, when you curate a music playlist, you fill the air with sound waves that speak to the fullness of the emotion that you share with the people who wrote these songs. When you hang photographs on the wall of your home, you create opportunities for the emotions that the photos represent to come to life. And the more chances we have to be in tune with our emotions, the more we will learn to be in tune with the emotions of others.

Art facilitates space to have emotional responses with one another. Emotional responses help create empathy. Empathy allows us to practice peace, together. To not set aside our differences but to push up against them as we sit down for dinner together on chairs that someone made, at a table someone crafted, with food someone prepared, from a recipe someone else wrote down. The song playing from the next room and the painting on the wall and the rug beneath our feet all hold stories worth knowing and sharing.

May we never become passive about making space for art in our lives. Let us dig to find music that challenges our perspectives, paintings that push us out of our worldviews, fiction that forces us out of our comfort zones. Art need not be only aesthetically pleasing. When we let art challenge us, we are able to feel our way into deep emotions that we may have forgotten, or possibly never even had language for. Art is an invitation to empathy. Empathy is the space where we are reminded that there is abundant room for what we are feeling. And when we sense we have permission to truly feel our emotions, we are free to put our guard down and breathe.

In times of heightened uncertainty, I believe it is critically important to emphasize that the connection between art and empathy is not restricted to oil painters, playwrights, and poets. In an interview on Jennifer Brown's podcast *The Will to Change*, Keesha Jean-Baptiste, senior vice president and chief talent officer at Hearst, shared her story of navigating crisis within the organization. At the beginning of the 2020 global pandemic, Jean-Baptiste started sending an internal weekly newsletter. She had already written and shared about a two-mile jog she had taken in honor of Ahmaud Arbery.

In her following newsletter, she shared, "I'm still struggling with the racial injustices in this country." In her interview with Jennifer Brown, she elaborated on this comment, describing how many members of the Hearst leadership team were unsure what to say to people of color during this time. When her coworkers said, "I'm afraid. I don't know what to say," this is what Jean-Baptiste said in response: "I heard from a few people on the leadership team and they said that that really hit them and that the initial outreach although might've been awkward on one end and maybe awkward to be the receiver, that it just taught them a lesson of how you can approach someone with humility but also compassion."[6]

Our words, our creations, our wonder, and our questions have the power to widen the reach of empathy—even when we are unsure of what the response will be. When we courageously share from the depth of our experiences, we end up pushing through the layers that keep us divided and, instead, connect on levels that only our souls know. Even when we just speak about what we're struggling with and problems we long to see solved, our stories are canvases that draw people in and invite them to feel into the raw emotions of the human being behind the words, and maybe even their own emotions too. This is the art of empathy.

THROUGH EMPATHY, WE . . .

Create Spaces Where People Feel Free to Exhale

If someone knows they're not going to be heard, they're unlikely to speak up. If they know their question might be misunderstood, they might avoid asking the question at all. Because of the many possibilities of what could go wrong, it's easier to stay at arm's length.

To practice peace in the collective, we need empathy. But empathy isn't always easy to dive into. Art, in all its many forms, is a powerful tool to help foster a sense of community. From storytelling to painting to music, art has the ability to get our attention and make us listen. Whether or not you consider your-self an artist, you can each use art to help foster a deeper sense of empathy within yourself and others. Share news articles *and also* the poetry of the people the article talks about. Stay informed by reading the news *and also* watching films that accurately portray the issues you study. Recommend music and books to those in your life who you think will enjoy them.

Art allows us to approach topics we might ordinarily be nervous about, whether we are afraid of questioning our own biases or saying the wrong thing. When we make space for art to flourish, we create mirrors for people to see themselves and exhale as they say, "Wow, I have felt that too."

Practice Peace by Telling New Stories

Sometimes the act of making art itself is a rebellion against a lack of empathy. As a descendant of African slaves in the US, after hundreds of years, I know that only a few generations of my family have been legally allowed to read and write. Knowing how hard it still is today for all children to receive equal access to education, I craft my words as an act of rebellion against antiliteracy laws that kept far too many from communicating in this way. In *African American Poetry: 250 Years of Struggle & Song*, editor Kevin Young wrote, "For African Americans, the very act of composing poetry proves a form of protest."[7]

There are many forces that will try to stop us from reading each other's stories, encountering one another's artwork, and then creating our own. But the more we persist, the more we create space for new stories to be written. We make room for others to inhale inspiration from the world around them and exhale their own paintings, songs, and stories . . . their own practice of peace.

THE MOVIE

Think of a movie you've watched that was based on historical events. Alternately, you could pick a film written or directed by someone from a different culture than you. Rewatch this movie and see if you gain any fresh insights. After the movie, research the actual events and see what new connections you can make. Some films bring in researchers and historians to consult throughout the filmmaking process, and there may be interviews you can watch to gain more understanding. Make notes of your findings. And now consider this: Who might you invite to watch this movie with you next time?

CONVERSATION

CHAPTER 9

CONVERSATION

In 2017 I invited people to share stories with me, and I would write poetry in response. I thought I would do this for a week or two, but here I am years later, and it's still a part of my regular writing practice.

While I do believe there are unique features to this ongoing project I've created, the idea of a poet writing with a particular person in mind is nothing new at all.

Gwendolyn Brooks wrote the line "we are each other's harvest" as a part of a poem to singer and activist Paul Robeson.[1]

Langston Hughes wrote "The Bitter River" in dedication to Charlie Lang and Ernest Green, who were "each fourteen years old when lynched together beneath the Shubuta Bridge over the Chickasawhay River in Mississippi, October 12th 1942."[2]

Rita Dove wrote her book of poems *Sonata Mulattica* about George Bridgetower, a biracial musician and friend of Beethoven to whom Beethoven dedicated Violin Sonata no. 9.

Ross Gay wrote "A Small Needful Fact" about the time of Eric Garner's life when he worked at the Parks and Recreation horticultural department.

These are the poems I come back to over and over. They are more than poems on pages. They are words that speak to the past, present, and future in a way that validates tender, often unspoken feelings that may take time to learn to say out loud. Through both Brooks's and Dove's poetry, I learn of history in a new way. From the poems of Hughes and Gay, I learn of futures stolen, lives ended too soon. And somehow, through these poems written for others, I see myself. Feelings of grief rise up from "The Bitter River," and comfort from "we are each other's harvest."

It's through poetry written for others that I am reminded that peace is not something we pursue off in the distance, all on our own, but something we practice together, through our words and actions.

Poems written for others are reminders that we are not only connected, but we also need each other to breathe new dreams and hopes for the future to life, and that is why I write them. If we want peace for the world, we cannot pursue it alone. We have to learn from each other, and we have to communicate with one another.

Prior to writing poems specifically for other people, I often felt stuck, not only as a writer but as a human being who wanted to do something meaningful in the world. It often seemed like no matter what I did, it was never enough. I would wonder if perhaps I felt this way because I didn't have enough influence or financial resources or wasn't business savvy enough. When I read the news headlines of the day, I felt even more helpless.

When I started to write for other people, I didn't think for a moment that what I did would have a larger impact on the world. But I noticed that when I wrote for one person at a time instead of trying to write for everyone in the world at once, I was speaking specifically to someone's story. And in doing so, I no longer felt like I was throwing words into the wind, hoping something would stick. Instead, I was in dialogue with an individual person with a real story.

This forever changed the way I wrote. Now when I write,

when I speak, or when I sing, I exhale for one. One person at a time. One story at a time.

There are a lot of issues in this world that I don't know how to fix, but I do know that to fix them, we have to listen. We have to stay in dialogue with one another. And this goes far beyond art and poetry.

Not too long ago, I had a menstrual cycle that wouldn't end. As the blood flow grew heavier and heavier each day, I eventually went to the doctor and found out I had a fibroid growing in my uterus. I ended up bleeding for several months with only a few short breaks in between. Eventually, I was able to have a myomectomy, a surgery to have the fibroid removed. This was my first time having surgery, and I wasn't prepared for the constant dialogue I would need to have with the surgeons, nurses, and medical staff.

As I tried to breathe through the process (while also having to wear a face mask the whole time), I also had to answer what felt like hundreds of questions, over and over. "What is your name? What is your date of birth? What kind of surgery are you having today? Do you need to go to the restroom? No? Okay, how about now?"

"Going to the restroom" ended up being a much bigger deal than I expected. As the surgeon successfully completed the surgery, I was informed that I couldn't go home until I went to the restroom, just to make sure everything was okay. The problem was, even though I felt like I needed to go to the restroom the entire time, I wasn't able to "go." This resulted in constantly calling for the nurse, who would help me up and down the hall each time.

Of course I don't remember what it feels like to be a newborn baby, but in that moment, I felt like one all over again. If I had a need, I first had to communicate it, then was completely reliant on someone else to respond to it. In this case, it was the nurse, who stood there waiting to see if she could help meet my needs.

This process went on for about three hours, and I couldn't help but feel like a nuisance to the nurse. Surely she had more important things to do than help me with my never-ending restroom requests.

"Thank you so much for your patience. I'm so sorry you have to keep helping me with the same thing over and over again," I eventually blurted as the nurse helped me to the restroom for what felt like the one hundredth time.

"No need to apologize," the nurse assured me. "This is what I'm here for. I'm here to listen. I'm here to help."

At the edge of her words, I exhaled, then stumbled into the restroom yet again. I didn't manage to "go" that time either, but I felt a little more free. I felt as though I had permission to let her know I was still struggling. And maybe this time I needed to drink the biggest cup of water she could find.

Outside of helping me, I have no idea what kind of day that nurse was having, but when she let me know she was "here to listen," it made all the difference.

Asking for help takes a lot of courage, but without someone there to listen, talk with you, and help you get the support you need, it is even harder. That day in the hospital, my conversations with the nurse were a part of my healing process. On that day, my fibroid was removed, and so was my fear of asking for help . . . because someone was attentive to my needs.

In the documentary *Coded Bias*, MIT Media Lab researcher Joy Buolamwini explored the many woes of facial recognition technology and algorithmic bias within the tech industry. Buolamwini visited residents of Brooklyn, New York, whose apartment complex of over seven hundred units had recently implemented facial recognition software to keep track of residents, in addition to other security measures that were already in place. The residents were concerned not only with the technology's ability to recognize Black faces but also with their right to privacy.[3] Buolamwini listened to the tenants and asked, "How can I help?" After her time spent with the tenants, Buolamwini appeared before Congress, where she presented in-depth research, including what she learned from the tenants themselves.[4]

I don't know a lot about algorithms, but I do know, from personal experience, that to dampen the effects of bias, we need to listen to one another. To create spaces where people feel free to breathe without being judged or fearing for their safety, we have to engage in conversation and do as Buolamwini did, asking, "How can I help?"

The more we listen, the more we see: yes, the world trembles with chaos, but that doesn't mean all hope is lost. We can still choose to seek peace, not only for ourselves or people around us but also for those who are already speaking out, ready to be heard. We can pay attention to stories that deserve attention, even if we have to go out of our way to listen. Whether we are researchers, poets, teachers, or gardeners, we can keep our hearts open to the ways that our work can help someone else find the freedom to breathe.

BY MAKING ROOM FOR CONVERSATION, WE CAN . . .

Make Room for Inspiration

I like to think that whenever I'm stuck and don't know what to say, write, or paint, it's time to listen. It's time to inhale. It's time to pay attention to someone else's story instead of my own. Sometimes that story will be shared in conversation, but often I read a book, watch a documentary, or listen to music in the background. When I get to the point where I have something to say in return, that is when I have the opportunity to join the conversation. Even if it's something as subtle as writing my thoughts in my journal, I am doing so as a part of a community and not a lone creator trying to produce something out of thin air. Sometimes ideas do seem to come out of nowhere, but most of the time inspiration comes from taking in real life. Real experiences. Real moments of connection with other people.

Writer Virginia Woolf once said, "Different people draw different words from me,"[5] and I think this is true, even for those who don't consider themselves writers. The more you engage with others, the more new thoughts and ideas will come to life. The more you will discover that perhaps when you feel restless and stuck, it's time to meet more people. One of the best ways to renew your own creativity is by listening and listening again. And then, when it's time, join the conversation with questions, poetry, or a generous hand.

Learn Something New

In the same way a book's bibliography can introduce you to a hundred new books, meeting a new person can introduce you to a hundred new stories. Because of one person's unique experiences and connections, they might share something that is entirely new to you. This connectivity is fascinating because, as poet Gwendolyn Brooks said, we are "each other's harvest."

Maybe your next big project at work will be birthed out of conversations with coworkers. Perhaps the next task you end up pouring your time and energy into will come from the needs in your community. Maybe your next art project will be less about an ambition to be a full-time creative and more about finding a way to honor the deep emotions you've been discussing with a friend.

Our conversations with family, friends, and our communities are wells of inspiration all on their own. They can remind us of the value of taking in our surroundings and then speaking up, creating, and helping when it's time.

Ask for Help

When you see an issue you want to fix but feel unable to, you may feel you've reached a dead end. But here's the thing about dead ends: you can turn back and trace the path that connects to other streets, other people. There are other ways of getting where you're trying to go; you might just need a little more help. Even if you feel like you should know your way around by now, there is no shame in asking for directions and guidance from others. Often we put too much pressure on ourselves to inhale all the right information and then exhale and execute what we've learned perfectly. But we are human, and we're allowed to seek help, even for what we feel we should be able to do on our own. We are allowed to pray about situations we thought we could handle alone. We are allowed to stay in conversation with others, staying inspired by staying connected.

THE HIGHLIGHT

Pick a book on your shelf where you remember highlighting a few passages. Or open your quote notebook (your bibliography) that you started creating in chapter 7. Get a sticky note or a small slip of paper and a pen. Return to a favorite quote and ask yourself, "What stood out to me about this passage?" Take a moment to think about it, and then consider what question you might ask the author about this passage. Maybe you'd ask them, "Well, how does this idea apply to this particular situation in my own life?" or, "Does this phrase have another layer of meaning?" Reflect on that question, and then when you're ready, take your sticky note and try to answer it yourself. Allow yourself to stumble your way to the possible answer. Let this be a moment of realizing how freeing a conversation can be, even if it's a conversation you're having with yourself on a small piece of paper. Even in this small way, conversation is a way of finding peace in knowing there is space for your thoughts, concerns, and questions.

CHAPTER 10

JOURNALING

There was a box of journals with my name written on it that I had been hesitant to open for quite some time. This box had traveled with me from my childhood home all the way around the country, including the many cities where my husband and I lived throughout our twenties. One day, cleaning out the closet when I was twenty-nine, I finally opened it. And there I found journals that dated back to when I was eight years old. I reluctantly flipped through the pages, cringing at the hilariously petty things I found worth writing down at the time. But there was also a lot of longing scribbled onto those pages. My jaw tightened as I read the words of a young girl who was so eager to find acceptance from her peers. My shoulders sagged as I read page after page of everything I wanted to say out loud but didn't know how.

At the same time, on these very same pages, this was also true: I was learning to name my feelings. I was learning to pay attention to the details of my story. I was creating a safe space to exhale after long days of taking it all in. I was practicing prayers that I didn't feel were polished enough for public spaces.

I may not always have had the right words to say in the moment, and I may have retreated to my bedroom with my notebook at times when I could have been more present to the people gathering downstairs, but I was practicing letting out all my thoughts and emotions. I was practicing speaking out loud. I was getting it out of my system. I was creating space when I wasn't finding it in the real world.

Journaling is so much more than a writing exercise. Sometimes putting words on paper will turn into poetry and prose, but most of the time the page serves as a space for thoughts. A place to just let them be.

Numerous studies have been done over the years on the mental health benefits of journaling. Therapists and behavior health specialists have found varying forms of writing to help manage anxiety and reduce stress.[1]

While teaching writing workshops, I often ask attendees about their relationship to journaling. Among the many answers, there is often a common thread: most of us have journals lying around that we've never finished or, in many cases, never even started. Life is busy, phones are convenient, and taking the time to sit with a pen and piece of paper can feel incredibly archaic in modern times. And people question whether there is enough time or even enough need to express our thoughts in this way.

Because simply backspacing or deleting anything we don't like has become second nature, physically scratching through something we want to rephrase or get rid of can feel strange and even jarring. The idea that we might spell a word incorrectly without autocorrect or a spell-check feature to instantly correct us might feel odd.

While in our minds journaling may seem like a nice form of expression, it can also feel like a daunting task that we don't have time for. I say this as someone who has managed to keep a journal for most of my life. Even though this is a practice I am incredibly familiar with, in modern times I'm sometimes finding it harder to justify and make time for. But as I flip through my old journals and see entire paragraphs scratched through (where I can still read the words beneath) and run-on sentences and unnecessary details that I wrote about at length, I also see the poetry it led to. I also see how amid all that, I was getting to know my own voice.

Meister Eckhart once said, "The deepest darkness becomes the clearest light,"[2] and I believe this applies to what we write as well. Keeping a physical journal where we write our fleeting, unpredictable thoughts with permanent black ink on a blank white page is an act of courage. Courage to dig deep into the words that you don't always feel you have the power or agency to say out loud. Words that help create language for all that is in your soul.

When I go back and read through old journals, I see nuances that would have been impossible for me to have picked up on at the time. I see days where my handwriting slipped off the page a bit because I was writing just before I fell asleep. Some days have prayers. Some don't. Some friendships I dedicated pages to, and some, only a sentence or two. Across many journals I see things that continue to appear: themes of desiring friendship and acceptance from peers, short stories about girls in new and unfamiliar settings, and floral doodles in the margins. Every time I go back and visit these journals, I learn something new.

When you look back on whatever you're writing about in this season, you will learn too. You might not walk away with some grand revelation about your life, but you will find a story of a living, breathing soul that was learning how to inhale and exhale through experiences. You will see moments when you were just doing your best to take in all the unpredictability life was tossing your way and also the moments when you simply needed to dedicate a few pages to air out your frustrations. You will look back, and again and again you will cringe, you will laugh, and you may even cry. And ultimately, all along, you will find you were practicing peace, even when you didn't realize it.

On the scale of what people have been through, I haven't had the wildest story. I haven't been through the worst things. But what I have been through, I have felt deeply. I have tasted the air of every moment I have lived vividly. I have felt the heat of the conversation on my skin. The snarl of the sarcasm. The cold shaft of dismissing. The pang in my chest of regret. I have felt it all. I have lived my whole life believing I was not sensitive, but the reality was that I was deeply sensitive. Affected by every little thing. Taking all of it in. I write this, after sitting here for a minute, trying to read, having been awakened by the sound of sirens. I'm going to try and go back to sleep.

—JOURNAL ENTRY, JUNE 2018

In the moment, I often question whether what I am expressing is of any value. I tilt my head to the side as I fill the page and wonder, "Why am I writing this down?" I can't always answer that question, but I can still move the pen across the page. As a result, I will be able to look back on these pages on another day and see these words in a new way. And when I do, sometimes I'll cringe, and I'll run across entire paragraphs that are pretty much gibberish to me at this point. But I will also find passages worth reflecting on. I'll find comfort in my own words. I'll see how God was crafting a beautiful story even though I couldn't see it at the time. And that alone gives me the courage to keep writing, because I know this process has value, even if it takes years to see how it all comes together.

Through Journaling, We . . .

Practice Peace by Recognizing We Have Something to Say

Rest in your God-breathed worth. Stop holding your breath,
hiding your gifts, ducking your head, dulling your roar,
distracting your soul, stilling your hands, quieting your voice,
and satiating your hunger with the lesser things of this world.

—SARAH BESSEY

There are many reasons why we might feel we do not have something to say. Perhaps we don't feel qualified, or maybe we consider someone else to be a much better storyteller. I once met a woman who commended me for sharing my story. I proceeded to ask about her own story, to which she replied, "Oh, I don't really have a story at all. There's nothing interesting about my life." I continued to ask questions about what growing up in northern Michigan was like. She told me about how many generations her family had been there and what she enjoyed about growing up there. Eventually, she cut herself off and said, "Wow, I guess I do have a story." I said I used to feel the same way, and it was only through people like her, commending me for sharing my story, that I realized I had something to say, even though I had initially regarded it as uninteresting and unworthy.

I love to exchange stories with other people. Whether it's someone I'm meeting for the first time or someone I've known for years, there is always room for new stories to come to life. Stories that are interesting, encouraging, or maybe even just worth sharing because it's a part of who we are. However, I have also had to learn that my story is worth spending time with even when no one else is around. I have something to say, even if the only person listening is my journal.

When I was journaling as a kid, I took this concept literally. With every new journal, I would dedicate at least two to three pages so the journal could get to know me as a person. I would bore the journal with all the mundane details of my life, such as what I ate for breakfast and how long I had had my own room. I would bring the journal up to speed about the books I was reading and the stories I was writing. To me, my journal was almost a journal with a capital *J*, a new friend in my life who was excited to get to know me. When I was about nine or so, I even cut off a small lock of my hair and taped it inside the journal so it could see what my hair looked like (fun fact: that lock of hair is still there).

Now, I'll admit that I'm a little embarrassed and even slightly creeped out by how much I treated my journal like a person who had walked into my life. But in some ways, I think I was on to something. I was okay with boring my journal to death. I was perfectly content with sharing the mundane details about life page after page, with only the slightest variation. And years later, those same details aren't so mundane anymore. What I ate for breakfast in 1998 and how I felt about the neighbors next door tell me so much more about my own story than I would ever gather from looking at a photograph.

By committing to be my ordinary self in my journal, I was practicing telling my story. I was learning to pay attention to the small details of my life that were worth being grateful for. I was slowly seeing that I had something to say, even if it started in the smallest way.

No matter how average, ordinary, or uninteresting you may feel your story is, you have something worth sharing, and your journal is a great place to practice speaking up. Your journal is an invitation to start the journey of recalling all the thoughts, feelings, and experiences that you've been breathing in and out all day. So here's to no longer holding your breath. Here's to making the brave choice to believe that you have experiences that are worthy of expression, even if only for the sake of gratitude for how far you have come or finding peace for your own life journey.

Practice Peace by Recognizing There Is Space to Share Our Stories

One of the purposes of journaling is to practice sharing your story. Practice finally exhaling everything you've been taking in and letting it come out however it needs to, in the form of a poem, a prayer, a letter, or a page in your journal that you don't even bother going back to read.

In our modern times, we face challenges of oversharing everywhere we turn, and there is an endless number of ways to share and platforms to share on. But here's what's true: Number one, no one tells the story like you do. And two, sharing online or on a public platform is not the only way. Sharing your story with a friend, therapist, or a journal is just as valid and necessary to process your thoughts and feelings and practice breathing out all that you've been taking in.

THE PRACTICE

THE JOURNAL

1. Look at your actual schedule, not your dream schedule, and identify where and how often you have approximately thirty minutes to yourself. Is it on Tuesday and Thursday mornings? Every evening around seven?

2. Once you've identified the days and times, put a journal and pen where you are most likely to be at that time of day. Is it the kitchen counter? Your bedside? The physical presence of the journal can remind you that there are pages to fill.

3. Open to the first page, or the nearest blank page, and cover the page in scribble. Yes, I'm talking toddler-style scribbling. I always start my journals with something that isn't pretty to go ahead and break myself out of the mindset that this is a place for only pretty thoughts. My journal is a place for expression. Honesty. Raw beauty. Sometimes it's pretty, but most of the time it isn't. My handwriting is all over the place. Sometimes I write in all caps, and sometimes I write in cursive. It's not consistent, and for the purpose of my journal, there is nothing wrong with that. Set the tone with imperfection. It only gets better from here.

4. If you can't quite bring yourself to scribble on the first page, another option is to go in the opposite direction and use a pattern by writing the same phrase over and over. The phrase can be something as simple as "My name is _____ and this is my journal," or "I'm not sure how I'll use this journal yet." The point of this exercise is to free yourself from a legalistic approach to filling this journal. Do what you need to do to feel your way into the journey. Allow your hand to brush against the paper. Find a pen you enjoy using. The more you write, the more you will discover what works for you and what doesn't, and in the beginning, a lot of it is in the mechanics.

5. When you're ready to write, start with the basics. Start with statements like the following:

> "I woke up at ___ a.m. today."
> "I drank a cup of ___."
> "I received a text message from ___."
> "I need to respond to this email from ___."
> "I hear ___ talking down the hall."

Starting this way may not be like writing a journal entry from the deepest, most expressive places of your soul. It may even feel like a logbook. But as Austin Kleon notes in *Steal Like an Artist*, "In the old days, a logbook was a place for sailors to keep track of how far they'd traveled, and that's exactly what you're doing—keeping track of how far your ship has sailed."[3] When you give yourself permission to write these seemingly boring details, you may realize that this list of ordinary events can easily become a gratitude list. You may see, as the days go on, that you can add a bit more about the text message you received. Perhaps you can write a sentence about how you are grateful to have that person in your life. Maybe you could write a paragraph describing the mug that holds the tea and why you've had it for all these years.

This is one of the many gifts of taking the time to write: You wind up appreciating things that a busy world convinced you were not worth noticing. You end up finding peace for parts of your story you didn't even realize you needed.

SILENCE

CHAPTER 11

SILENCE

A few years ago in Atlanta, I was pulling into a parking spot at a restaurant, and my sister, who was in the passenger seat, gestured to the window of the car beside me and said, "Morgan, look at the way this dog is looking at us!"

In the car next to us, the person in the driver's seat was sitting there scrolling on their phone, but their dog was in the passenger seat and was staring at us with eyes so focused, they almost seemed human. The dog sat there in perfect stillness, just watching without blinking. Even as we moved, the dog remained still, looking in our direction, almost as if to say, "I've been waiting for you."

It was slightly eerie, but the way our sense of humor works, my sister and I burst into laughter and we couldn't stop. I couldn't even take my seat belt off as I curled over the steering wheel with laughter. Every few seconds, we looked over to discover the dog still staring at us, and that made us laugh even harder. As my sister and I laughed with our full bodies, the person in the driver's seat did not budge or look our way at any point.

We wondered if eventually the dog would bark or make some movement to get their owner's attention, but after sitting there for who knows how long, laughing until we couldn't breathe, we realized that this dog had no interest in giving us anything but an intense dedication to stillness and silence. We laughed about this for hours. The friends we were joining in the restaurant politely laughed with us since this was probably one of those "you had to be there" moments that we couldn't let go of.

To this day, I can still see this dog's face gazing at me through the window. I had never seen a dog be so incredibly still and silent for so long and with such intense focus. Who knows, maybe they learned it from their owner.

What I learned from this dog that night was the power of stillness and silence. This dog's doing nothing but staring stirred up more curiosity and laughter within me than I ever would have expected, and I laughed harder than I had in a long time.

My mother grew up in a home where she was the youngest of six. She recently told me that her mother, my grandmother, in a busy house filled with children, would often say she wanted some peace and quiet. Considering that I grew up hearing my mother use the same phrase, this makes sense to me, and now I use it too. From this, I can see that in my family, we've been after some peace and quiet for a while.

The phrase *awkward silence* applies to many scenarios because in a noisy world, silence itself can feel incredibly awkward. Because silence doesn't usually come easily in modern times, it's something we have to pursue and work our way into. Only in that pursuit of quiet will silent moments feel more natural.

For most of us, silence might as well be a mystical place out in the forest somewhere that is accessible only if we take the day off in search of it. From the buzzing sounds of notifications on our phones to the busyness of the traffic outside, the world gets moving early in the morning and doesn't stop until the late-night hours, if it stops at all. Even sounds of life in our own homes, such as children playing, roommates watching movies in the next room, or someone walking around opening and closing doors, can keep us from the peace and quiet we seek.

Sometimes, asking for peace and quiet can feel a bit odd when you know that everyone else is already minding their own business and not trying to disturb you. We accept the noisiness as part of life, and we carry on with everyone and everything else. But inevitably, something happens that brings us to a place where everything else quiets down and we are left with nothing more than what's happening in the present moment. Sometimes it's something funny, like an intensely focused dog, and sometimes it's something more serious. A phone call that throws off the schedule for the whole week. An accident on the interstate that delays us by an hour. A news headline that changes not only the course of the day but the course of history.

We never know what's going to send us off course. We never know what will make us feel like we are stuck at some point in the cycle of life and all we can do is sit there and take it in. But here's what we can do: we can practice. We can practice making room for silence in our daily lives. This way, when a time comes that deserves silence and reflection, we can be at peace with the quiet.

I found myself sharing this message with a few friends who didn't know what to say in the wake of the tragic loss of George Floyd's life. I remember sharing with each other how angry we were at how many Black lives had to be lost for people to finally pay attention to this historic problem. As Black people, my friends and I often felt pressured to rise up and do the emotional labor of providing words that were informative, poetic, and activating all at once. But the truth was, we were tired. We were tired of seeing far too many people not take this seriously for too long. So I said to my friends, "You don't need to have the words right now. You've been speaking about this for years."

In the wake of the protests of late spring and summer of 2020, I found myself saying this to myself as well. I needed to acknowledge that I was angry and grieved and that I did not have to feel shame if I did not have the words right away. I could seek moments of silence, even if it was nothing more than spending hours away from social media for the sake of my own mental health. I am grateful for the activists and educators who were anything but silent, and I also had moments when I wasn't quiet and spoke openly and directly in the best way I knew how. At the same time, even though I felt so much pressure to constantly have something to say, I had to learn to intentionally seek moments of peace and quiet.

When it came time to speak, the silence helped me nurture a part of my voice that I might not have known had I kept on speaking. On the last day of May, I uploaded a song on social media that I wrote called "One Breath at a Time." Amid everything that was going on, even as I was angry, the first thing I shared was a song:

I'm out of answers, I'm out of breath,
I'm about to lose the small hope I had left.
I'm tired of traveling, longing for home.
But it's so far away, has it been too long?

Is this what it looks like when you've reached the end?
Do I accept all my losses 'cause there's nothing to win?
Or do I
keep believing
when I'm losing control,
there is still room
to be still my soul.

In the following days, the song was included on NPR's list of songs called "The New Sounds of Protest and Hope."[1] What rose up out of the silence ended up connecting with others in a way I hadn't expected. I will carry on seeking justice, breathing in and breathing out, entering silence and using my voice at the pace I was meant to.

THROUGH SILENCE, WE . . .

Make Room for the Delightfully Unexpected

Whether slightly humorous or wildly revolutionary, all kinds of new ideas, insights, and thoughts await us each day. But the noisier the day is, the harder it can be for those thoughts to materialize. By making room for silence, we make room for the new and delightfully unexpected. And we don't have to sit in silence for hours and hours in order for this to happen. Pace yourself into silence, slowly becoming more and more comfortable with the quiet.

Accept That It's Okay Not to Know What to Say

Silence teaches us that it is okay not to know what to say. In troubled times, our thinking minds are inclined to work overtime, looking for ways to solve a problem. Even when we mean well, sometimes the best thing to do is just to be present. When someone in your life suffers an unimaginable loss, it is likely that more than they need the right words, they need someone who is willing to sit there with them in silence, ready to listen whenever they're ready to speak. By making room for silence in your life, you make room for others to feel like they are free to simply be. They will know you as the one who will be there, even if you don't have the words. It matters to have friends like that.

Practice Peace by Speaking Up When the Time Is Right

The more talk, the less truth;
the wise measure their words.

—Proverbs 10:19 MSG

Embracing silence doesn't mean staying silent forever. But through silence, we learn to choose our words wisely. Through silence, we learn that words, while a useful part of communication, are one of many forms. Silence also teaches us to listen, observe, pay closer attention. Silence teaches us to inhale in a mindful way. It also teaches us to exhale and let things go without always having to say something. Be attentive to the timing of when you should speak and when you should be silent.

THE PRACTICE

THE HOUR

Which hour is the quietest of your day? When are you least likely to hear the cars outside or people moving throughout the house? If you don't have an hour that is completely quiet, that's okay. Simply try to find the time when there's less noise than usual. Perhaps there's an hour that includes fifteen minutes in the bathtub at night or the few minutes when you are steeping your tea before you head back to work. When you arrive at that hour, check in with your body. What do you need? Let the silence speak.

CHAPTER 12

REST

Since ancient times, there has been a natural rhythm to the day, marked by the sunrise and sunset. As the sun rose in the sky, we would rise, and as the sun set, we settled down. Of course, that changed with the development of electricity and the invention of the light bulb. These changes brought many gifts and modern conveniences, of course, but artificial light does come with its woes.

In an article for the BBC, journalist Linda Geddes wrote about her experience with living for several weeks without artificial light. Geddes, who also wrote a book on this topic, describes in detail not only her personal experience but also the scientific research that looks at how artificial light affects everything from our mental state to our sleeping habits. In the article, Nayantara Santhi, a research fellow at the Surrey Sleep Research Centre, notes that "light has a powerful non-visual effect on our body and mind."[1] Santhi has also done research on how artificial evening light can delay when we go to sleep.

As Geddes traveled through her days and nights, avoiding her exposure to artificial light, she and her family made many adjustments throughout the "dark weeks" to be able to see after the sun was gone from the sky. Geddes used candles throughout her home, and though candlelight proved to make preparing dinner difficult, it created a more relaxing environment for everyone, and with time they even enjoyed it. Geddes noted, "I'm also learning to embrace the long winter nights: seeing the season as an opportunity to make the house cozy with candles rather than bemoaning the darkness."[2]

Growing up, I saw candles as nothing more than what you pulled out of the closet when the electricity went out. I didn't think of them until that moment when we would suddenly be sitting in sheer darkness and my mom would spring up to fumble her way to the candles. When they were lit, the room was instantly filled with a warm and vibrant yet subtle glow.

I have a friend with a robust candle collection, and it wasn't until I was visiting her and she gave me one to take home that I realized candles are for far more than emergencies and special occasions. There's a whole lifetime of moments for which they can be used. Since then I have started lighting candles just because. I keep at least one candle in every room of the house and light them at various times. As the sun sets, I feel inclined to turn off the lights and let the candlelight fill the room, even if only for a moment.

While I haven't mastered the ancient practice of living without artificial light, the candle is a reminder that the invitation is there. Beyond the artificial light pouring down from the bulbs in our ceilings and lamps and the brightness beaming from our devices, the dim flicker of light from the candle is a reminder that maybe, for all the excess light we have, a flicker is just enough.

As we all know, the longer the candle burns, the more the wax begins to melt. The pool of wax grows larger and larger, and eventually you have to blow the candle out. The wax eventually settles down and dries up.

What I love about dried candle wax is that it doesn't settle back into place exactly as it was. If you look closely, you'll see that the wax has taken on a new shape. I have one candle that has three wicks spread out in a large bowl. The more I've burned this candle, the more each wick seems to carve out its own space, creating what looks like a little canyon landscape, complete with rock ridges so defined that an ant could scale them if it wanted to. But every time I light the candle, the landscape changes a bit. And I know that eventually the candle will be no more.

As morbid as it may sound, this is true of life. We don't live in these bodies forever. Every day, we grow older. Our bodies change. The world changes around us. Nothing is exactly the same as it was yesterday, and we do ourselves a favor when we take notice.

However, this reality can be tough to remember in daily life. With electricity alone, we have been able to extend our days significantly. And whether it's professional or recreational, we can have more jam-packed, productive days. But if you've ever had a busy schedule, you know this: more doesn't always mean better. While extended days have their benefits, they can also make it more difficult to rest. They can cause us to forget to stop and breathe.

I write these very words in a room with artificial light, and I also have a candle burning. While the average incandescent light bulb can keep going for around a thousand hours, the candle can't burn that long, and I can't either.

When I think about the burnout I've experienced in my life, I often feel as though I've failed in some way. I wonder if I should've been able to keep up the pace a little longer. I measure myself as though I'm a light bulb that could literally stay on for thousands of hours. I forget that, as a human being, I can only do so much for so long.

Keeping a candle around is a reminder of the natural rhythms that are easy to forget in our 24/7 world. When we're on the verge of burnout, it's a sign that we need a break, even though we may feel pressure to keep going. And if we don't expect the candle to burn all day, we shouldn't expect that of ourselves either.

As we live with the tension of artificial and natural light in our daily lives, let us remember the original intention for natural light—that we would pace ourselves with the rising and setting of the sun.

Media Distinctio

In Western music, a musical notation sign called a "rest" indicates when to pause from playing your instrument. The rests vary in length and are determined by the beats in the music. We didn't always have these symbols to indicate where to stop. The method of measuring these rests didn't come around until the thirteenth century. Before then, there were other ways of finding room for the rests. In *Silence, Music, Silent Music*, musicologist Emma Hornby gives insight on how Benedictine monks would notate their music using a form of punctuation called *media distinctio*.

> In choral psalmody, one half of the community would sing odd verses, and the other would sing even ones.
>
> In the middle of each verse, there was a pause for taking breath, the *media distinctio*. . . .
>
> The *media distinctio* was considered to be a ceremonial pause. . . . It sometimes served as an architectural pause, lasting until the echo of the previous pitch had died away; the length of the pause depended on the acoustics of the building. . . . An important aspect of the *media distinctio* was the unity it embodied: the unity of the monastery breathing and singing together; and the reflection that gave of the unity of the heavenly host.[3]

What I love about this practice is that the monks made use of the actual space they were in to determine where the musical rests should be. They sang. They let the words and music fill the space. And then they paused. They let the sound fill the room, giving it space before they sang again. They didn't rush from one line to the next. They let their voices fill the room, and they let the silence fill it too. There was room for both.

Many of us feel as though our lives are defined by the way we rush from one thing to the next. We respond to one email, and two more come in. We pay one bill, but three more are waiting. We finish one task, but the list of tasks has grown. We get one day off from work, but we pay for it the next day with everything we have to catch up on.

Media distinctio is a reminder that despite the pressure to rush from one thing to the next, there is room to take a breath. It's a pause that reminds us who we are outside of what we do and what we achieve. This is what it means to rest. It is here we will find freedom. It is here we will find peace.

We often feel like we have to earn rest. Many of us live with the unspoken idea that only those who have worked to earn their keep should be allowed to rest.

I once asked my blog readers this question: What was your relationship with the word *rest* when you were growing up? The answers varied, but I lost count of the ones that sounded like this:

"I didn't feel like I was allowed to rest."
"Rest was viewed as something for the weak."
"I never saw anyone in my family resting."
"Resting meant that you weren't being productive."

There is no doubt that many of us have struggled to cultivate a healthy relationship with rest. Whether because of busyness, guilt, or a disquieted mind, rest is hard to come by, especially on a consistent basis. I still struggle to rest regularly and constantly have to remind myself of my need for rest. Often my body tells me of my need for rest before my mind can catch up. The yawn is a signal. The heaviness in my eyelids and the sudden need to stretch are signals too. But what about when the rest we need isn't sleep but to take a break from processing our thoughts? Rest from traveling? From doing the things we love? From consuming information online?

If I inhale a lot of information during the day and know I need a break, I put down my phone and leave it at that—only to pick it up ten minutes later and enter the cycle again without realizing it. If I sense that I need to rest, it's easier to write about it or go searching the internet for new poems on rest than to back away from the desk and actually rest. Rest is a relatively simple concept, and yet it's something many of us struggle to incorporate into our daily lives.

I have begun to pursue rest by seeking out specific places to rest. One obvious place to begin thinking about rest is my bed. When it is time to sleep, I have the privilege of having a bed that allows me to do that each night. When my back touches the mattress and my head touches the pillow, I am in the mindset and the literal posture for rest.

Beyond the rest I find while in bed, I have found that if a day is filled with too much noise, I can open the window and look out at the trees for five minutes. Even if I can still hear the cars whizzing by on the street behind me or the kids walking home from school, there that tree stands, silently, profoundly, a symbol of simply being present amid all the noise. Literally rooted, a tree is, as Wendell Berry once wrote, the "grace of the world."[4]

Nature gives me landmarks that symbolize rest. I associate the pine tree in my backyard with the pine tree in my childhood backyard, where I would take a book and go sit at its trunk. I associate the feeling of my bare feet touching the grass with a comforting flat surface, such as a bed, a symbol of stillness. When the sky is blue and clear of clouds, I look up and am reminded that in the same way the sky is breathing free of clouds right now, I too can slow down and do nothing more than breathe. And rest.

Another reason I take the time to connect blue sky with rest is because every space in my home is multipurpose. I don't have a room that's just for resting in the middle of the day, and if I did, I wonder how often I'd use it. Instead, I connect with nature and find rest there.

I love that nature has built-in rhythms of rest, and when I take part in them, even for five minutes, I am reminded that while the human-made world is always in a rush from one thing to the next, the natural world does not live by those rules.

Ironically, in our modern world, it takes some work to define what rest is and what it isn't. Here are a few things that rest is not:

- Catching up on rest on the weekends. Studies show that trying to catch up over the weekend isn't restful, nor does it help with sleep deprivation.[5]
- Anything that still requires a high level of mental activity, such as responding to messages, doing chores, or running errands. Even if we're not on the clock with our jobs, our minds still have to process a lot of information that keeps us from fully resting.[6]
- Vacations, for even when they are restful at the moment, the positive effects wear off within a few days.[7]

I've also learned to look to objects in my home to take cues to rest. We associate all kinds of meanings with certain objects, so why not associate some of them with rest? To find room for sustainable rest, we can slow down and look at our daily surroundings as well as notice the sights and smells and textures that draw us into rest. Here are some ideas:

- Turning on calming music, even while you're still wrapping up projects
- Playing natural sounds as you get ready for bed
- Drinking warm chamomile or lavender tea
- Going for a brisk walk around the neighborhood to process a deep thought, which could even lead you to forget about the thought and then come back inside, ready to rest
- Changing into comfortable clothing
- Reading something on a physical page, not a digital one
- Debriefing the day in a physical journal
- Taking the cue from the tiredness you feel after a phone call (even an exciting one!) as a moment to pause, sit on the couch, and do absolutely nothing

One of the best indicators that you are rested is when suddenly you're not in a hurry. Far too many of us have been conditioned to worry relentlessly about time. We all have access to clocks, and we also have internal clocks fighting to get our attention each day. Because staying present to the moment can be a challenge for many of us, we can use everyday objects to gently prompt us.

The objects in your living space say a lot about you and your personality, and they may also represent what draws you into a restful state. Maybe, just maybe, you didn't purchase that photograph only because it was pretty. Maybe there's something about the mountain or the cactus or coastline in it that reminds you to be still. Maybe something about the scent of a particular candle, the texture of a pillow, or the trusty elasticity of your favorite sweatpants makes you feel like you can take a deep breath, if just for a moment.

Suddenly, with a candle lit, trusted sweatpants on, and nature sounds playing softly in the background, you're not worried about time, and something in your body softens and you exhale: "You know what . . . those emails can wait." And all is well. You can rest in the grace that is finding you in this moment.

I am learning to be grateful for the moments when the house is quiet, even if the stillness lasts only ten minutes. I also take time to notice when the sunset is noticeably more colorful than usual, and I linger in its presence, letting the golden rays find my skin as I watch those same rays light up the color of the changing leaves. In that gratitude, I rest. I welcome the chance to read for thirty minutes even though I wish I had an hour. I am thankful for the beauty of the walk around the neighborhood even though I need a vacation. I am grateful, amid all that crowds my restless mind, for any moment when I encounter spaciousness—the unrushed natural rhythms of the world, or, as author Alan Fadling wrote, rest in the "unhurry [that is] rooted in Creation."[8]

Where you find gratitude, you might find rest. When you find small glimmers of light that remind you just to relish in the goodness of the moment, maybe you are syncing in the rhythms of grace in ways you never have before. And perhaps, in those rhythms, you are reminded of the beat of your heart, and with the beat of your heart, you are reminded to breathe it all in, breathe it all out. Pause amid the gritty reality of life, and rest in the in-between.

To rest is to practice peace.

Through Rest, We . . .

Honor the Natural Rhythms of Our Bodies

Whenever rest feels far away, we can hold on to the fact that natural rhythms of rest are already built within us. We just have to find our way back to them. You can turn to the sun rising above your head or the leaves of the deciduous trees falling to the ground and think, "In the same way there is a rhythm to nature, I have rhythms too." Give yourself grace to work your way back into that knowledge over and over again.

Resist the Pressure to Always Be "On"

From one direction or the other, we will likely encounter pressure to always be "on," whether that's at work, church, or with family. But we inevitably find that even if we lean in the direction of extroversion, we still need our rest. It is important to remember that the pressure to be "on" sometimes comes from a good place. Our friend is going through a tough time, and we don't want to worry her with our stress, so we keep a smile on. We have family members who rely on us, and we know that if we take a moment to rest, we won't meet their needs. So we keep going and going until eventually we burn out. When you feel you need rest but it's hard to stop, recognize that this may be an area where you need a bit more practice . . . and there's no shame in that.

Learn to Live Unhurried

In a modern, technological world, it is only through practice that we learn to live unhurried. We don't yet know the lasting effects that access to endless information and technology will have on our lives. So when slowing down, resting, and not feeling guilty for it feels like an uphill battle, that's because it *is* an uphill battle. We've never been here before, and we are learning as we go. Keep this in mind: you're not the only one living with the tension of your natural rhythms and the hurried pace humans have created. We're in this together, and we can practice learning to rest, together.

THE PRACTICE

THE SUNSET

As the sun sets, notice the artificial light sources around you. What devices, lamps, or ceiling fans are on? Ask yourself, "Which of these do I need right now? Which of them am I able to turn off? Could I replace one light source with a candle?"

GRIEF

CHAPTER 13

GRIEF

first met Buster on a Saturday morning in a shopping mall parking lot on Highway 78. I was out shopping with my dad when we came upon a family whose dog had puppies, and they were giving them away, right there in the parking lot. I remember the family gathered around their pickup truck, petting the puppies and talking to the small crowd of people that had gathered around to see the litter of puppies prancing around. The puppies were a mixed breed, and even though they were the same size and had similar faces, each dog was a different color. My eight-year-old self couldn't resist getting a closer look as we walked through the parking lot, and like a magnet, the small puppies' barks drew me in. With my dad beside me, I was barely tall enough to see into the bed of the truck where the puppies were, but I saw enough to spy one little black puppy off in the corner, all alone.

"Daddy! Can we get a puppy? Can we get that one?" I said, pointing to the black puppy.

I must say, I don't remember any of the exchange that happened after that. But I guess, at some point, the answer to this question was yes because the next thing I knew, we were heading home with my first puppy. I couldn't believe it. I had asked and I had received. Before we were even home, I decided his name would be Buster, for no other reason than I liked the name. I rubbed my hand along his smooth black fur and imagined all the tricks I would teach him and all the adventures we'd go on in the backyard. At that time, I was learning about dog breeds, and I had learned about black Labrador retrievers. I thought they were the most beautiful dogs, and I was certain that Buster had to be at least part Labrador. I took that one little bit of information and ran with it, pouring myself into the one dog breed book I had, trying to learn every possible thing there was to learn about Buster's possible ancestry.

One of the things I loved about Buster was his calm demeanor. As a kid, I often felt that other kids had the capacity to be a lot more energetic than I was, and I felt the same about the few dogs I knew. I struggled to keep up and often felt like I was lagging behind everyone else. But Buster seemed okay with my pace. He didn't mind the times when I was quiet and all I wanted to do was walk around the backyard, observing rocks, sticks, and fallen leaves.

In those days with Buster, walking around the backyard is the memory that plays back most clearly, as if it happened yesterday. Buster showed me the power of a quiet, loyal companion and how it's okay to just be, no matter how many times you feel the pressure to keep up with everyone else. Buster showed me what a Saturday morning could be, how calming and peaceful it could be. And though I didn't have the words for it back then, in my heart I was grateful.

A few Saturday mornings later, I walked into the living room to see my dad with his head hanging low. He noticed me standing there, and I saw sadness in his eyes. "Morgan, I'm not sure what happened but . . . Buster has passed away."

I stood there perfectly still for what felt like an eternity. Whatever magnet had pulled me in the direction of that truck to meet Buster was now pulling me toward the ground. I tried to move my legs, my lips, my neck, but nothing moved.

My dad was the one to take Buster to be properly buried. I knew that my dad, who had grown up with his own "Buster," loved Buster as much as I did and that I could trust him to make sure Buster got the best send off. As I stood there, unable to move, I knew I wouldn't get to say goodbye. I couldn't bring myself to see Buster in that state. I didn't understand why his life ended so soon. I thought back to the Labrador paragraph in the dog breed book. Had I missed some important information? Had I missed the signs?

As I grew older, I shifted from feeling guilty to shame for grieving Buster. Yes, I had lost my dog, but many others had lost so much more. I had attended more than a few funerals, as my parents, both ministers, were often the ones reading the eulogies or leading prayers at the burial sites. In many ways, it didn't feel right to grieve Buster in a world where people lost parents, children, and siblings. As I looked over to my parents and my sister, I couldn't imagine what that must be like. And yet, even to this day, I miss Buster.

In 2001 I attended a funeral that hit much closer to home. My mom lost her brother, my uncle, whom we would see multiple times a week. I was eleven years old, and I grieved the loss of my uncle, yet at the same time, I couldn't shake the idea that my mom had lost her brother. Her brother, who was about the same distance apart in age from my mom as me and my sister are, lived only a few minutes down the street.

As we drove by his neighborhood in the weeks and months that followed, I would hold my breath, feeling sadness knowing that we would no longer be turning down that street like we used to. And as we drove on, we were usually headed toward Highway

78, where we would pass the parking lot where I first met Buster. I would hold my breath again.

Unfortunately, in the years following, my family lost a series of family members whom I knew and saw regularly. With every loss, I carried feelings of grief while also telling myself to hold it together because my loss wasn't as significant as that of those who had lost their husband or child.

Nearly two decades after I lost Buster, I was driving through the Atlanta area running errands. I had moved away from Atlanta by this time, but I was back visiting and driving a rental car around areas that I frequented over the years. I found myself on the road that led to where my uncle had lived. Then I was at the traffic light where I'd turn to go see another family member that had passed away. Eventually, I found myself on Highway 78, where I first said hello to Buster. As I drove by the parking lot, my eyes welled up with tears. For the first time, I cried every last tear over the loss of Buster. I pulled into the edge of the parking lot, opposite of where the family in the pickup truck had been with the puppies. I couldn't bring myself any closer to the location—where I sat was close enough. Close enough to grieve.

Through that experience I realized that grief at a distance is still grief. Unfortunately, there will always be those who have been closer to grief and have lost more than I could ever imagine, but that does not mean I am not allowed to grieve at all. I am free to take in every memory, every moment of connection. And I am still allowed to exhale, in the form of tears, when it hurts to say goodbye.

Because of COVID-19, many people have attended a funeral service via a video call. Far too many people have said goodbye to parents, children, siblings, cousins, and friends through a screen. It is estimated that roughly one in five Americans lost a friend or family member to COVID-19.[1] Grieving at a distance is something that too many have had to learn over the past few years, and yet grieving is not bound by space and time.

Grief is a mighty wave that can wash up on the shores of everyday life, no matter how long it's been since the loss. And often what brings that wave to shore is the parking lot or the song or the photograph that reminds you of not only the initial loss but also the million other things you've lost since then. As I cried at the sight of a parking lot, I was grieving everything I loved and lost from that moment onward. I was also grieving all the years when I didn't know how to let myself mourn in a world that seems to be sinking with losses greater than the ones I have personally known.

When I grieve, I am finally exhaling all the memories I inhaled over the years, both great and small. And even though nothing will ever be the same, I am still free to sit in that parking lot and inhale all over again and hold that memory as long as I want to. For all the sorrow that followed that day in the parking lot, there was joy too. And I can return as often as I want and remember both sides of the story.

In this life, we will experience loss, and we will also experience love. We won't know when and where, and that's the hard part. But we are allowed to inhale and exhale every moment for what it is. Cry when we need to. Laugh when we need to. And ultimately, allow ourselves to feel what we need to feel.

It is important that we acknowledge and make space for those who have faced significant losses. But their grief doesn't diminish our own. We are allowed to let the tears fall. We must continue to discover and remind one another—in the grace of parking lots, journal pages, therapists' offices, and conversations with friends—there is room to exhale. There is room to remember the good and to grieve.

Through Grief, We . . .

Practice Peace by Letting It All Out

For a hundred reasons, we might feel the pressure to hold it all in and be strong instead of fully grieving. Maybe you're the oldest child, trying to hold everyone together. Perhaps people see you as the "strong one," and you don't feel as though you have the freedom to fully mourn as others do. Maybe no one has shown you what healthy grief looks like. Perhaps you feel like you should be done grieving by now. If peace is a river, grace is the force that keeps the river flowing, making room for water—no matter how much—to find its way into the watercourse. There's room in the mighty river of peace to feel everything, so let any tears of despair or outcries of anger find their place. No matter who is watching. No matter who has made you feel like it wasn't okay, even if that person was you. There is room to let it all out. Feel what you need to feel. And breathe.

Practice Peace by Not Discounting Our Losses

When we encounter someone who has lost more than we have, that doesn't invalidate our need to grieve. In the same way we could never measure someone's joy based on what they have, we can't measure someone's grief based on their loss. One person's grief simply cannot be compared to another's. Grief is deep sorrow. There is no ranking. There is no one-upping. Don't discount your losses or push aside your pain. You are allowed to grieve, right here, right now.

Honor the Lives of Those We Love

When we are able to, we keep the memory of those we love alive by doing what they loved, talking about times we shared with them, keeping their photographs around, or thinking of them when a certain song comes on or when we visit a place we used to travel to with them. This is not always easy, but whenever we are ready, the opportunities are there. Since my mother-in-law passed away, as a family, we have spent quiet time by the waterfront near her childhood home on the island of Oahu. On the shelf where I keep many of my favorite journals, I also keep my grandfather's Bible with his name engraved in it. It's been two decades since my uncle passed away. He was hilarious and the life of the party, and we still talk about his style of joke-telling. These moments don't make the pain of loss go away, but they can remind us of all we gained in having these beautiful souls in our lives.

The Practice

The Landscape

Think of a landscape that brings you to a state of calm reflection. Is it the mountains? The forest? The shoreline? Close your eyes and travel to this place. What does the sky look like today? Is the wind blowing? Is the air cold or warm? Is this somewhere you've traveled with someone you love? Or a place you wish you could have traveled to together? One of the beautiful elements of landscape is its vastness. No matter the landform's visible features, the landscape is wide, with room to roam, to dream, to grieve, and to breathe. Travel to that landscape in your mind as often as your imagination allows you to.

CHAPTER 14

HEALING

When I think of the word *healing*, I think of a time-lapse video I once saw of a wound on a finger healing. I, along with many others in the comment section, found myself surprised by how dry and crusted the wound looked as it healed. It got worse before it got better.

I have struggled with the word *healing* for a long time. Growing up with a sister who has a neurological condition, I had seen church people use this word to claim that if she let them pray, they could heal her if only she had enough faith. We encountered those who seemed set on "fixing" her the minute after finding out about her condition, as if Christians were not allowed to have someone like her in their midst.

For a long time after this, I tensed up at the word. When I began to write for other people's stories, occasionally I would be asked about healing, but I never knew what to say. I was still trying to find healing from the damage the word *healing* had done.

One day the word *healing* came out in a poem I was writing for someone. It fell onto the page before I could stop it:

> I am worthy
> of the time it takes
> to do the things
> that heal my heart.

As I prepared to send the poem to the person I wrote it for, I almost rewrote the *heal* out of it. I couldn't imagine putting this person in the same situation my sister had been in, even in the smallest way. I went back and read the sender's original message. Then it made sense why something within me loosened enough to include this word: she had mentioned the word *healing* several times herself. She had shared with me about her love and her losses, and that's exactly what she was after: healing. Suddenly, I felt free to write about healing in this poem. Her mentioning healing was permission for me to reflect it back to her. Also, she had written to me about wounds of the heart, the kind of healing that you don't just see work itself out like a finger cut binding back together in a time-lapse video.

In *Everything Happens for a Reason: And Other Lies I've Loved*, Kate Bowler generously shares her story of reckoning with mortality when she was diagnosed with stage IV colon cancer. In the book, she offers a list with this title: Absolutely Never Say This to People Experiencing Terrible Times: A Short List. In response to the phrase *everything happens for a reason*, she says, "I've had hundreds of people tell me the reason for my cancer. . . . When someone is drowning, the only thing worse than failing to throw them a life presever is handing them a reason."[1] Bowler then goes on to offer us a short list of what we can try instead. This list includes "I'd love to bring you a meal. Can I email you?" and "Can I give you a hug?" Bowler gives a window into what it feels like to be on the receiving end of these words and how sometimes the small, practical things are what we need. What I dearly love about this list is how much it involves coming back into the body and into the nonsensationalized practicality of providing balm for wounds.

I once sat in a church service where the pastor declared that we were not doing enough healing and we needed to do it quickly. He referenced Jesus walking and healing the sick, and I couldn't help but wonder, "Okay . . . and what about the walking around part? That seems to be a common thread in these Jesus stories . . . walking around and just being with people first." I am not trying to minimize where and how healing happens, but I can't help but notice that we as humans don't spend much time listening to others' stories, walking alongside them, and allowing for slow healing.

Sometimes I am told that in my work I don't challenge people to change enough. That I don't push hard enough. I receive emails about how I need to be more direct about what people need to fix. But the more time I spend listening to people's stories and reading them as they enter my inbox, the more I find that, for the most part, people already receive a lot of messages about what they're not doing. Many are already on the path of realizing what's not working, and they're actively seeking a new direction. It's not that conversations about change aren't necessary. There's much to be said about poor decisions and all the issues they cause. At the same time, when I am writing for people that I don't know, people I have never swapped stories with, I am extra careful with my words. As I inhale what they have shared with me, I exhale with a mindset that even with all they've shared, I only know so much about this person. When someone has kindly invited me into their story, I can give them the gift of my presence. Often, I have found that when someone reaches out, they're not looking for advice. They desire what every other human being is looking for in one way or another—to be seen.

Stories, especially stories of tragedy and trauma that we can't fix, have a way of disarming us. They also can leave us feeling like we have failed if we can't make everything better. Yet we are free, at any given time, to get down to the bottom of it all and focus on what connects us. We can pause before we speak and say to ourselves, "We are two human beings who, for whatever reason, have crossed paths to be here for this moment. How can I be present to this other soul?"

I think it is far too easy to drastically underestimate just how much people need to be seen. On any social network, you will see friends and strangers alike sharing post after post. At first glance, it can seem to be for vanity. Why are all these people posting so much? Don't they have other things to do? Do they even have lives outside of social media? But after decades of an ever-increasing, ever-loudening pulse of mass communication, we have all been dealt the task of trying to navigate a global, growing machine that none of us ever asked for. It's easy to look at a handful of teenagers or irresponsible grown-ups in a viral video and say, "There's no hope for humanity." But sometimes we have to sift through the noise to hear the real message.

This is one of the main reasons I have chosen to share poetry and artwork on the internet over the past few years. I don't think my work has all the answers by any means, but I do believe that in an ever-evolving digital landscape that makes it easy to consume messages about what we don't have, what we can't figure out, and who we're not, it is critical that we also have messages that remind us of what we do have, what we do know, and who we are: human beings who still have the capacity to enter into love, grace, and peace.

A slower, more considerate look at our current landscape finds this: a lot of hurting people who have been dealt something they don't know how to fix. Sitting with ourselves in the silence has become painfully difficult. Our wounds go deep. We need healing. And it is not too late to pursue healing, collective healing, throughout the seasons and cycles of life.

Let's breathe in the air of each other's stories and find compassion and patience and grace for one another. And if we don't get it all right immediately, we can remind each other that we're still practicing. Day by day. Breath by breath. That's how we heal. That's how we grow.

Through Healing, We . . .

Practice Peace by Not Putting Time Constraints on the Healing Process

No two wounds heal the same. Some take longer to heal than others. Some heal and leave no mark, while others scab over and leave a scar. And then there are those wounds we know are there but can't physically touch. The ones that leave us with questions: "Why is this taking so long?" "Will I ever heal?" There is no shame in not having the answers. We practice peace by accepting that slowness does not equate to ineffectiveness. Healing differently from someone else doesn't mean you're healing wrong. For some wounds, "healing" might feel like finally finding a friend who understands. It might sound like the rumble of the ocean waves that makes you forget about everything else. It might taste like the morning air that reminds you of your freedom to breathe.

Practice Peace by Having Empathy for Others

When we understand that wounds heal differently and at different paces, we are able to have empathy for those who are healing in their own way. Knowing there is no one right way to heal can help us be a healing presence. Be the one who isn't concerned with rushing everything along. Become someone others can turn to because they know you're not going to rush to fix them.

THE BREATH

What matters more than anything in the healing process is that you are alive. While you may have a recovery plan mapped out on the calendar, the most important things are the inhales and exhales. Whatever your relationship is to progress right now—whether it's slower than expected or you're trekking right along, may you never underestimate the power of each breath. If all you do today is take mindful inhales and exhales, that matters more than you know.

LETTING IT OUT

CHAPTER 15

LETTING IT OUT

It took me almost twenty years to tell my parents about the time I was kicked in the face at a sleepover. In short, I didn't want to get the girl in trouble. Furthermore, I felt that if she found out I told, there would be some kind of retaliation. She would tell the other kids, and I would feel even more like an outsider than I already did. Also, I didn't want my parents to feel bad. I knew they would rush to resolve this issue, but the thought of having all that attention on the situation brought me a lot of anxiety. Even while I was telling them the story two decades later at age twenty-seven, the frustration and pain on their faces was as if it had happened to me just yesterday.

The incident took place in the living room, where we had all our sleeping bags in a circle. Somehow my sleeping bag wasn't perfectly in the circle, and I was trying to find my way back in. I started to scoot the sleeping bag forward when a girl I'll call "K" kicked me in the face. I assumed it was an accident; perhaps she didn't realize I was trying to put my sleeping bag into the circle. Only a dim light was coming from the kitchen, so I assumed she didn't see me.

I scooted backward in my sleeping bag and tried to enter the circle again, this time careful not to get anywhere near K's feet. "Can I come in?" I whispered, gently squeezing my way into the circle. The other girls were talking among one another in the circle, but I wasn't sure if they heard me. So I inched my way forward, glimpsing enough of their faces to see where I might fit between K and another girl. As I scooted forward a little more, K looked back in my direction and we made eye contact. She turned on her side and proceeded to kick me directly in the face as a way to push me back outside the circle.

She did this swiftly, without a single grunt, and from what I could see in the dim light, none of the other girls turned around. I sat there in disbelief, too shocked to cry or move. I lay awake for some time before I fell asleep, and I avoided K at all costs from that moment forward.

As I told my parents this story, they stood there in shock, frustrated and saddened for me. But as I told them, I found my own shoulders loosening. My jaw became less tight. Seven-year-old me was present in that moment, and she was grateful that I spoke up.

Telling this story all these years later taught me that keeping quiet when you've been hurt is not the way into peace. In the moment, we may feel like we are inconveniencing someone with our pain. We may fear the repercussions of what might happen if that person finds out we told the truth.

I am angry and stand in solidarity with everyone who has experienced bullying, assault, or abuse, and it is my hope that we can live in a world where practicing peace looks like less violence and more support for victims. I share my story because while it was one moment of childhood bullying, it's never too late to talk about the importance of letting out our experiences, fears, or feelings. We should all feel free to exhale in a safe space where we are allowed to have boundaries. It's never justified for anyone to hurt us, no matter how big or small the issue may seem.

Not too long before I told my parents this story, I was in a coffee shop in my hometown, and of all people, K was in the queue a couple of people before me. I hadn't seen her in years. The second

I realized it was her, I started to dart in the other direction. But I was too late. K had finished placing her order and had noticed me. Looking in my direction, she said loudly, "Morgan! Is that you?"

I stood there like a deer in headlights. I was seven years old again, unsure of what to make of this moment.

"It's been so long!" she said. In her eyes, I saw not even the slightest glimpse of aggression. It seemed likely that she had forgotten about that moment at the sleepover all those years ago.

I took a step back and ended the interaction quickly. I couldn't mentally process what was happening, but my body was telling me to leave, and I did just that. I walked away.

Processing the encounter later that day was what led me to share the sleepover story with my parents. Even though it happened years ago, telling someone felt good. It was a practice in breathing out, which seemed impossible to do all those years ago.

Moving forward, I became more aware of thoughts I had been holding in for whatever reason. Some of these were much smaller and even silly, such as one day telling my mom that I didn't like yellow rice growing up, but I ate it because I knew she loved it, or telling my husband that on a sensory level I didn't have the capacity to watch action films and I'd rather watch a baking show instead. It's small admissions like this that still take practice to say out loud. They take practice because I have spent many years holding them in.

I have found that practicing peace looks a lot like learning to let it out. Learning to trust that even though it doesn't always feel like it at the time, there are people out there who are willing to support you and also seek justice on your behalf when necessary.

Whether what we're holding in is small or great, we have to practice letting it out. We have to practice breathing deep. It's difficult work, but for the sake of our collective and individual safety and well-being, it's worth it.

Through Letting It Out, We . . .

Practice Peace by Speaking Up

Sometimes it will take everything within us to speak up. Telling the truth may require the longest, most mindful exhale we've ever released. For victims and survivors of abuse and violence, it takes great courage to speak up, to talk about something that never should have happened in the first place. It can't be said enough: speaking up matters. You are worthy of love, support, and justice.

Practice Peace by Not Minimizing Our Hurt

When we consider all the ways people have been hurt, even within our own families and communities, at times we may feel we are not worthy of the same tenderness or care because what others have been through seems more significant. Even when we accept our hurt as valid, we may feel like sharing it with others burdens them or that seeking help will make us look weak. But these are simply not true. Pursuing help may take great courage, but it is always worth it.

Allow Others to Help

Sometimes we may not reach out because those in our immediate circles have dismissed our pain. We may have been legitimately hurt, and yet we've been told or made to feel that it's our fault and our responsibility to make the problem go away. Because of this, we may forget that other people are out there. There are friends, therapists, clergy members, doctors, lawyers, and others who will say "I see you," and can help you find peace in letting it out—and letting someone in.

THE CALL

Whom in your contact list do you feel free to call for no other reason than to say hello? If you can think of only one person, that's okay. (And if you can't think of anyone at all, that's okay too. As long as you're breathing, there's still hope that eventually you'll have that person). Give this person a call just because. Practice reaching out, even though you don't know the outcome. If making phone calls like this makes you anxious, prepare yourself for possible scenarios. Maybe they won't answer and the call will go to voicemail. Could you leave a message that says, "I was just calling to say hello"? Perhaps they'll answer and ask, "What's up?" to which you could reply, "Just calling for no reason other than to say hi." Take a deep breath and place the call.

NOTE: Instead of calling, you could send a text message. Use whatever method you're most comfortable with. What matters is to practice reaching out.

LETTING IT GO

CHAPTER 16

LETTING IT GO

Sometimes practicing peace looks like letting go, especially letting go of how we thought things should be. One of the clearest examples of this has been in my marriage to my husband, Patrick. We've been married for over ten years, and in addition to being my spouse, Patrick is also my business partner. When I began sharing my poetry and artwork online, it was Patrick who turned to me and said, "What if we turned your artwork into prints?" He also did all the research on finding the right printing partner, deciding what envelopes we needed for shipping, and figuring out how much inventory we should order each month. Even though my online shop is filled with art that I make, I can't take credit for the business side of it. It wasn't until Patrick came up with the idea to sell prints that I was able to breathe deep and finally feel like a small business owner and he was able to leave his job in construction to operate the shop full-time.

When we tell people we work together, we have been commended for being able to partner with our spouse to grow a business. While I say thank you, I also have to acknowledge two things: One, it took time. It took nearly a decade of trying and failing before we worked well together. Two, the only way we were able to make this business relationship work was by learning to let go . . . and this was largely on my part.

I have to admit that I am extremely particular about my art. I notice right away when the off-white comes out with a hint of yellow instead of a hint of pink. Even when others say, "Morgan, no one will notice that," I respond and say, "But I notice it." I wish I could say I was laid back when it comes to art, but I'm not. I know the exact pixels my digital paintbrush needs to be to get the right swoosh of cerulean across the bottom third of the page. I notice when cerulean is starting to look more like teal and the clash this might create. I notice when lettering is slightly off-center and there's not enough negative space around the text's border. I feel like my attention to detail in this area is one of my strengths as an artist. But it can keep me from peace when it comes to relationships.

When Patrick came to me with the idea to sell some of my art as prints, I tilted my head to the side, widened my mouth in a forced, open grin, and said, "Eh . . ." (which is sometimes my indirect way of saying no.) Immediately, I thought about how I'd have to crop the art in ways I might not want to, for example, to become an eight-by-ten-inch print. I worried about all the ways that the printing process could go wrong and how the colors might be off. And since I make a lot of art and wasn't really creating in series at the time, I had no idea how to create a collection.

"Okay, what if I tried to select the prints and make the collection?" Patrick asked me.

Grudgingly, I agreed. He returned half an hour later with his picks, and I immediately had an opinion on why each one wouldn't be a good pick and which ones I would choose instead. He listened and then went back to selecting. This time he returned with choices that included mine. Suddenly, we were talking about creating this collection of prints . . . this collection I didn't even think could exist half an hour ago. In that moment, Patrick's patience became a pathway for me to see what I had been missing: I had been standing in my own way. For years I had struggled to earn a sustainable income as an artist. And when I say sustainable, I simply mean not paycheck to paycheck. While Patrick worked long hours in construction with a three-hour round-trip commute each day, I managed to scrape by with just enough freelance work. But working from gig to gig was stressful for me and a strain on our finances. I knew something had to change, but in my mind, my art wasn't ready yet. I was afraid to order inventory. What if no one bought anything? What if we wasted time and money? It became easier to make up excuses, to pretend I was reluctant to create this shop because of my artistic knowledge and eye for aesthetics. But in reality, I was afraid. I was afraid of failing. I was afraid of the unknown.

As we sat there picking prints, love looked like letting go of old ideas. Even though I was the "creative one" in the relationship, Patrick had worthy ideas too. Even though planning and organizing weren't my strengths, that didn't mean I shouldn't have a plan for what I had created. When I was trying to hold all the pieces of my art career in my hands, telling myself that no one would want to support me as an artist by making a purchase, I was stuck on the inhale. But in that moment, seeing the possibility for growth—even though it looked different than what I thought it would—caused me to realize how much fear I had been holding in. And when I started to let go of that fear, I let go into love. Love showed me that sometimes we can practice peace by listening and letting someone into the space we are convinced that no one would understand. And it was there I could exhale.

Shortly after, we launched the prints, and they sold out within the first day. Suddenly, we had orders to fill and a small business in the making. I had been holding my breath for so long. So afraid to let others into what I was doing. So afraid to ask someone to buy a print for fear that I might appear desperate or face rejection. And yet as I saw the fruit of Patrick's plan, I was humbly reminded of the importance of letting go. The exhale. The act of letting someone else help for a change. Letting go of the reins of control and allowing something new to come to life.

This letting go caused a huge shift in our lives. At the time all this was happening, I was also seven months pregnant and facing the reality that our jobs would have to support another person soon. Also, we needed health insurance, and when you work for yourself, that isn't always easy to come by. By making this change with the shop, we were finally able to get health care. By the time our son was born, we had managed to set up a full-time business in our apartment.

Life was pretty hectic in those early months as we had to take care of a newborn, purchase product, and fulfill orders around the clock. We alternated tasks, and as my body took longer than expected to heal, I would often become frustrated with myself for the things I couldn't physically do.

In short, even as our immediate financial worries began to take a back seat to raising a newborn and starting a business at the same time, it was only through God showing me how to let go that I was able to make it through.

I had an image in my mind of what a "mompreneur" should look like, and I'll tell you, she looked a lot more put together than I did. As I sat there breastfeeding with one hand and responding to customer emails with the other, and feeling the aftershock of the major life event that had taken place in my body, I was exhausted and overwhelmed. I realized that all I could do was let go. Let go of how I thought life should be in this moment and accept it for what it was. And in doing so, I was able to fully love the moment for what it was. Fully love being with my little one. Fully love finally being able to work from home with my husband, as a team. Fully love that I got to make art and share it and receive love from people around the world who wanted to support it. No, life wasn't perfect. It was exhausting, and I dealt with physical pain for a long while. At the same time, every moment was filled with love. And it was more than enough.

Through Letting Go, We . . .

Embrace Humility

Whenever we have something we're proud of, it becomes a bright light in our lives. But sometimes the brightness can cause us to forget about the shadows. Just because we're proud of our ability to be creative or to come up with new ideas or to be a leader doesn't take away the fact that we must leave room for growth. Humility is accepting that even when we feel like we have a good understanding of who we are, we can usually still learn something from those who love us.

Release the Need to Be in Control

Life becomes extra stressful when we remember that we are not in control. This is why we have to practice letting go of our need for control, even in the smallest ways. One of the simplest ways we can do this is by taking a deep breath when we become frustrated with someone or something we can't control. We can inhale slowly and exhale slowly. Of course this won't change the outcome or immediately put us in control of the situation, but taking the time to breathe can help us regulate our thoughts and emotions. Then we can see that while we might not be able to control every outcome, we can control our breath. And by controlling our breath, we can carry on, trusting that we can know peace even when we're not in control.

Free Ourselves from Expectations

For several months after giving birth, I was insecure about not looking like I thought I would. I had been warned about the lack of sleep and lack of energy I might have, but I hadn't been told how long it would take for my body to heal. I didn't anticipate how hard it would be to move around the house comfortably, let alone take care of an infant and run a business. Those first few months looked nothing like I thought they would, and I still look back in awe of how I made it through. At the same time, I know this to be true: every single day, I was learning how to slow down, breathe deep, and let go of how I thought this stage of life was supposed to be. For me, this letting go was physically painful and emotionally draining. However, on the other side of my severed expectations was room—room to breathe and let each moment be what it needed to be.

When we are finally able to let go of expectations, we are finally able to make room for new ways of thinking. We are able to make room to see that when we were struggling, perhaps we were also growing in strength. When we were challenged by unwanted outcomes, we were also growing in our capacity to feel and express our emotions. Letting go is anything but easy, but we can trust that on the other side there is space to breathe and room to encounter peace beyond our understanding.

THE ANONYMOUS GOOD DEED

Think of a good deed you would normally like to be recognized for, and instead do it anonymously. If you take pride in being a leader, then maybe give tips to a colleague on a project, which might result in them getting the credit instead of you. If you take pride in being creative, then perhaps create something and share it online without putting your name on it. Practice doing something good for the sake of doing good. Practice letting go of the need to see how it all turns out or how you'll be perceived. Practice letting go for the sake of remembering the real reason why you love what you do.

PLANNING

CHAPTER 17

PLANNING

I find a lot of value in looking back. This is especially true when it comes to my work. I am easily distracted. I can have a clear idea of where I want to take a project or how I want to set up my workflow, and then I read someone else's story and suddenly wonder if I need to try to incorporate their philosophy or approach. I read something in a book about beauty or wisdom, and instantly I question whether I should focus on those topics instead of my own. Looking back helps me see what worked and what didn't. Looking back allows me to be at peace with everything I tried and failed. I am able to see that in the seasons where I was pacing myself and producing results I was satisfied with, there was no secret formula or specific creative philosophy that made it happen. What I see is that I was being present. I was present to my emotions. I was present to the people who so generously shared their stories with me. That was when I made my best work, not when I was trying to follow a perfect plan—mine or anyone else's.

Looking back has helped me plan for the future. When I reread my most recent journal, I saw that I dedicated about twenty pages, once again, to trying to come up with the perfect workflow for myself. Part of me laughed at the sight of this, and the other part realized that even though I never figured out the workflow, I survived. I finished the projects I was working on at that time. Maybe I didn't get to everything on the list, but when I wasn't working, I was resting. I was going for walks. Spending time with my family. When I reflect on the plans that didn't come together, I look at the other plans that didn't come together, and I realize there was still priceless significance in my days.

As I keep going through the journal, I see where I made notes after listening to a podcast or reading a book. I see bullet point notes, and then after the points, I wrote everything I couldn't quite fit into bullet points. That's the good stuff. That's the true heart of why I do what I do. And that's more important than any single plan.

The point is, making a plan is a bridge to figuring out the pulse of what you want to do. A plan helps you identify motivations and think through ways forward, but that doesn't mean you have to attach your identity to it. If you're ever hesitant to make a plan for fear that it might not work out, go ahead and release yourself from that pressure. A plan is just a plan. That's all it is.

Before making a plan, it is important to know your goal, your intentions. An intention is "something that you want and plan to do."[1] An intention is the heart of the plan, getting down to why you even want to do this in the first place. Knowing your intentions means that even if the plans fall through, you're still a part of something greater. You're free to come back to this later. Refine. Reshape. Try again.

This is all a part of practicing peace. We breathe in all the possibilities of what could be and then exhale, releasing the need to control the outcomes and letting go of any shame we may feel when we have to start telling people that the plan has changed, that things didn't work out.

I have to hold on to this mindset every day. For most of my adult life, I have been a self-employed creative. My husband (now also an independent contractor) and I spent many years living paycheck to paycheck. As much as I love the arts, this way of living was not a choice. I applied to many jobs over the years that never really worked out. I now know that what we experienced wasn't uncommon for our generation, but back then I remember feeling ashamed and less-than when compared with my peers. I would meet people our age who worked in medicine and tech and tell myself, "See, they're doing real work. What are you doing, Morgan? Making music? Making art? And you're broke?"

Even though I was never strong in math and science, these voices in my head were loud enough to convince me that I should find a way to go back to school for a career that was more respectable. While I tried to create my next bullet point, my new outline for the future, one of the few things that helped me take my mind off my worries was my iPad. I downloaded art apps and started doodling and attempting to make art for the first time in a decade. It was four years after that small beginning, which I didn't even realize was a beginning, that Patrick suggested we start an online shop.

Even with our progress and all that's gone right for our business, those voices still linger. I still find myself asking questions like, "What am I doing all of this for again? Am I a writer who makes art, or an artist who writes? Is this worth it?" Maybe to some these seem like silly questions, but for me they scratch at the layers of feeling worthless that I am still healing from. I sometimes still long for a clear trajectory—if I just did X, then it would lead to Y, and everything would be fine.

In one way or another, we all feel the pull between wanting to control the little details we hope fall into place and living a life of surrender to the process. I know I am not the only one who wonders what they're actually doing every day and if and how it matters. Surely I'm not the only one who lives with the tension of wanting to mix things up and yet also yearning for steady rhythms and stability.

I want to take a moment for those of you who aren't quite sure what you're supposed to be doing with your lives. For the ones who want to make plans but aren't sure if they're the right ones. For the ones who want to practice peace on this long and winding path called life but simultaneously wonder if they're walking toward a dead end. I want to be another traveler on the road who says, "Yeah, I get that feeling too." Rather than focusing on getting every detail right for an unknown future, you can go deeper into the details of the story that's already being written.

What words keep coming up in your journal?

What memories do you keep coming back to?

What questions do you keep asking yourself in the middle of the day?

What places in the past do you long for? Why do you think that is? What does that longing say about what you might want to do in the future?

There's so much richness in your story already. And there is still time to learn from where you've been. You can go in a new direction. You can look back and take a closer look at what did and didn't work in the past.

Looking back can be a form of gratitude. When we look back and allow ourselves to see what was good, we see that no matter the failures, we have plenty to be grateful for. We have traveled this road with grace. Not perfectly, but with grace. We can be undone by life and all its unpredictability and keep going. And all those roads we've traveled and all those mountains we've climbed follow us along the way. The wisdom you've already gathered before you ever start making that new list, the courage you cultivated long before you ever dream the new dream, the stories of resilience passed down through the generations, the moments of vulnerability in a relationship where it didn't end how you thought it would—it's all right here. You learned and you grew from all of it. All by grace.

Make plans considering everything that led you here. Make plans that allow you to continue adding to the threads of what has already been woven together in your life. Make plans as a form of commitment. Pen your lists with the intention of learning and growing, no matter what. Make plans knowing that even though you still have a long way to go, you have already come so far. You are still inhaling and exhaling, taking in new experiences that inspire and challenge you. Now it is a matter of how you choose to move forward. Will you allow dreams and ideas to flow out of you while simultaneously surrendering to trust? All that is to come might end up surprising you.

Even if you ultimately end up going a different direction than originally expected, what matters is that you already know what it means to breathe deep in the wild of your unknowns and keep going anyway. Let your plans point you to the bigger picture so that you can be reminded that a little list does not determine your worth. Remember the intentions behind what you do. You've got this. You've been on your way here for a long time.

Three Steps to Planning with Intention

1. Notice what gets most of your attention. Even note what makes you angry. Focus on the stories you've heard and the experiences you've lived through. It may help to review your own journals, your screenshots, and even your internet search history. They can tell you something about what pulls on your heartstrings. Unfortunately, we live

in a world where people may be inclined to participate in a certain cause or movement for the wrong reasons—for clout, financial gain, or to help soothe their guilt. Make plans for the future based on the change you would like to see.

If any recent experiences cause you to think deeply about the kind of work you want to do, write about them. Talk about these issues in real life. Join forces with people who are already doing the work. Read as much literature as possible. Take these steps so you can cultivate a posture of deep listening in a world where distractions are ruthless. Let wisdom and grace remind you that you don't have to process everything right away. Identify the places where you can listen and learn. Start with one or two issues that move your heart.

2. Think about accomplishments you are most proud of and what steps you had to take to reach those goals. Also reflect on activities you enjoy that don't drain you. This is important because if you're an introvert, maybe you need to free yourself from an overabundance of social activities that drain you. If being stuck at a desk drains you, then perhaps don't center your plan on writing a book, even if you feel that's what you should do. Often we make plans for the future based on "shoulds." We focus on what our peer group or social circles deem worthy and valuable. If you've ever felt pressured to go through with a plan for this reason, you already know how draining that can be. Now is the time to make plans considering how you're wired.

3. After you have written your plans for the future, write down your hopes and your prayers and your heart for the present. Beneath the layers of those plans, what faces came

to mind when you considered why you'd like to accomplish these things? Give yourself permission to feel into the deep layers of the heart behind these plans. When you look back at this list, whether or not the plan was successful, you will find that the threads of your life connected to other threads. You continued to be present with all you had in every season. You kept going.

Through Planning, We . . .

Get to the Heart of What's Important to Us

Our plans for the future reveal more than what we hope to do. They also reveal what's important to us. At the center of a plan to move to a new city could be a heart for adventure. At the center of a plan to work for a particular organization could be a heart to make a difference in your community. At the center of a plan to have a family of your own could be a heart to experience love in an intimate way.

Take a look at the heart of your plan. Even while you wait to see how your plan falls into place, you can still nurture the heart of the plan today. You can do meaningful work and make meaningful connections even while you wait. By focusing on the heart, you'll discover that you can still breathe deep and know peace without knowing what comes next.

See That Our Successes and Failures Do Not Define Us

We are humbled by failed plans, and we are proud of the successful ones. But no matter which outcome we face, that is only one of many in our lives. We are not defined by our successes, nor are we defined by our failures. We are not defined by what we do but by who we are. This can be a difficult concept to grasp because what we do determines where we live, how we eat, and who we know. Even when we aren't working to pay bills or completing tasks to move forward in life, we are still living, breathing human beings who are worthy of love, no matter our successes and failures. So inhale and exhale knowing that you are worthy of love, right here, as you are.

THE PRACTICE

THE LIST

Make a list of all the future possibilities for your life. Include alternatives that aren't exciting dreams or well-thought-out plans, such as, "I could end up staying in this line of work for another decade" or "I could shift into the research aspect of what I do." Leave the list alone for a week. Come back and pay attention to your emotions as you read through it.

TRUSTING

CHAPTER 18

TRUSTING

R ight after I graduated from college, I worked as an admissions counselor. I would often ask prospective students which major interested them, which is a common question in US college settings. If I could go back and change one thing, I would ask a different set of questions: "Which topics interest you? What are you interested in exploring? Does anything on this list of entry-level courses stand out to you?"

I would ask these questions because I'd regularly meet a student who, after a deep sigh, would nearly whisper, "I'm undecided." They uttered the words almost as though it were a secret they were reluctant to confess. By this point they probably knew what was on the other side of a decision regarding their major: a well-meaning grown-up telling them everything they could do, going on and on about subjects they would excel in and career fields that would provide them financial security and happiness. And yet here they were, choosing to enter college with the word *UNDECLARED* written out, in bold letters, on all their student documentation.

Even though I started out thinking I knew what I wanted to study, I would end up falling into that same category. I changed my major from music to English, back to music, to undecided, and back to English. Interestingly enough, it's that "undeclared" section of my college story that led to an unexpected shift in my life.

During the semester when I was undeclared, I moved back home from my college campus and enrolled at a local community college to finish the second half of my second year. I had left the music program, having lost my scholarship after failing a biology class, and I figured I could take a few required classes to bide the time and figure out what to do next. In my required American literature class, we were assigned to write a poem. It was that poem that led my professor to say, "Morgan, I think you have something here."

That conversation led me back to being an English major. I declared my major with a bold ellipsis: "Maybe there's something here . . ."

There was nearly an entire decade between that moment and the one when I began to call myself a "poet." When I look back, it seems that all the signs were there: all the literature classes I loved taking, my memorization of lines of T. S. Eliot's "The Love Song of J. Alfred Prufrock," the music lyrics that I would dissect long after the album was finished playing. But it was going to take time to see it . . . and there was nothing wrong with that.

Even though I was in the middle of this unknown, trying to figure out what I would do with my life, I was learning simply how to be in this life. I was learning to inhale everything I needed to inhale, even if it was just for a required class. I was learning to exhale with all that I had, even if it was an assignment someone gave me. I was learning to be still, right where I was. According to my own standard, living at home and going to community college was considered "going nowhere," and yet even though I couldn't see it then, living slowly, doing the same set of tasks every day, taught me (the long way, of course) that you don't have to know what you're going to "do" to be still and let moments within the uncertainty shape you. It has ultimately been through moments like this that I have been able to find peace in the waiting.

Periods of waiting are often marked by not knowing what to do or feeling like you're doing the wrong thing.

Are you wasting your time?

Are you putting your time and energy in the right place?

Is it all worth it?

We don't give ourselves permission to be "undeclared," and others don't give us that permission either. We're expected to know what we're doing, and if we don't, we'd better figure it out fast.

I have found that the times when I feel most directionless are when I'm pressuring myself to make my life look like someone else's. When I admiringly look at someone else's contribution to their industry or when they speak confidently about the work they do, I hold up a mirror and start examining what I need to fix so I can be a little more like them. But when I inevitably discover that I will never be just like them because I can only be me, I exhale and let myself simply be. I back away from the desk. I go outside and let the sunlight find me, and I remind myself of what the sundial knows—that, yes, at some parts of the day, light will cast a shadow on what feels like a stone plate of my life. And yet that is only one part of the cycle. I am still free to embrace stillness and let the sun do its work through me, one hour at a time.

When I look back at my Tuesday schedule from that undeclared term all those years ago, I can feel the weight of it:

8:00 a.m.–8:50 a.m.—Biology
9:00 a.m.–9:50 a.m.—Political Science
11:00 a.m.–11:50 a.m.—American Literature
1:00 p.m.–1:50 p.m.—Ethics
6:00 p.m.–9:00 p.m.—Art Appreciation II

Political science class at nine o'clock with a lively professor who welcomed debates (during an election year, I might add) is a lot to take in. Having ethics class immediately after lunch, in a small, shadowy classroom with even smaller desks, is quite a bite to digest. Yet it was all a part of embracing the unanticipated stillness that I found when I had to move back home when I didn't want to. I showed up every day, like millions of students before me, and sat down to listen to lectures I might never remember. To turn in assignments that didn't always feel purposeful. To wake up early in the morning for a test that would drain me of all my energy for the day.

I left that term in the same way I left many other terms in my life—not able to make sense of every single thing I learned. I still felt directionless, yet somehow I kept going.

Over and over in my life, I seem to come back to this lesson: being at peace is knowing that you don't always have to know the details of every step ahead to ultimately end up where you were meant to be.

A few years ago, I was running late for jury duty. For some reason it had slipped my mind until the last possible minute, and I darted out the door and headed downtown. As I weaved my way through traffic, all I could think about was the parallel parking situation ahead of me, and I hoped I would make it into the courthouse in time. I had never done jury duty before, but I knew it was something you didn't want to be late to.

I was sitting at a red light, trying to think about how many more green lights I could afford to miss before I'd be late. I had about seven minutes and two lights up ahead, and I was in a busy downtown area. The math wasn't looking good.

As I looked ahead, I heard, "Hello! Excuse me!" coming from the car next to me.

I looked to my right, and a woman was rolling down her window, trying to get my attention.

I reluctantly rolled down the window, thinking about how this was the worst possible time to have a conversation of any kind.

"I'm wondering . . . do you know how to get to Commerce Drive?"

As it turned out, I did know exactly how to get to Commerce Drive, but my brain couldn't compute the directions in time. Suddenly, the light turned green, and without even thinking, I said, "Um, yeah! Follow me!"

Just like that, I was leading the driver to Commerce Drive, knowing good and well that even though Commerce Drive ran adjacent to where I needed to go, this would probably put me more than a few minutes out of the way. But at this point I couldn't let her down. What if she was running late too?

Finally, we made it to Commerce Drive, and I waved at the driver as she found her parallel parking spot. I looked at the clock and had about a minute and a half to park before I was officially late. Miraculously, someone was pulling out of the coveted non-parallel parking spots in front of the courthouse. I grabbed it immediately, and there was another small miracle: plenty of time left on the parking meter.

I darted across the parking lot with all I had, arriving at the security checkpoint completely out of breath. I made my way into the room where the jurors were supposed to meet, and I handed my jury duty card and driver's license over to someone sitting at the desk.

"Oh, you're good," he said, handing me my card.

"Okay, great, so where do I go next?" I said.

"No, you're good. We don't need you for jury duty anymore. You can go home."

I was still out of breath and frazzled at this point. I stood there for a few seconds trying to collect my thoughts. All the stress and anxiety it took to get here, suddenly pointless.

I made my way outside, stepping onto the square where the courthouse sits with other office buildings and restaurants. I noticed a burrito place off in the corner and decided to head in. This was supposed to be one of those weeks where I stuck to my eating-out budget, but after the kind of morning I had, I allowed myself to break the rule.

I walked through the queue, ordering my burrito, still tired and dressed in business casual for no reason at all. As I reached the end of the line and was getting ready to pay the cashier, a voice came from the back: "Hey! Her meal is free!" I looked up, and it was the woman I had helped find Commerce Drive. "Yeah, her meal is free . . . she helped me get here today."

I noticed the woman was in a slightly different uniform than everyone else, and I assumed that maybe she was a new manager at this location and had been trying to find her way here. I thanked her and accepted my burrito in disbelief.

Sitting on a bench outside the restaurant, enjoying my burrito, I wondered, "Did I come all this way for a free burrito? Or to help someone get to their first day on the job?" Either way, I decided that whatever the reason, it was worth the trip. I had been redirected, and as stressful as it was in the moment, in the end I was fine. Sitting there between the courthouse and the burrito place, enjoying my unexpected breakfast, I was fully convinced that everything had worked out how it was meant to.

I wish I could say I always feel this way when being redirected, but the truth is that bigger redirections are harder to process. But every now and then, this burrito experience comes to mind, and I take it as a cue to trust. To trust that if bigger redirections come my way and I am told to go home and that I'm not needed, even before I've settled in and found my seat, I'm free to leave and be at peace, knowing there's more to see. I can trust that God has more to show me. No, it won't be what I expected, but I will look back and realize it was still worth the trip.

By Trusting, We . . .

Practice Peace by Looking at the Map

When we are learning to trust, we are surrendering the need to know what will happen. We are learning to accept the possibility of many different outcomes. By trusting, we are looking at the map while simultaneously knowing that once we're on the road, the journey may look different. There will be detours, delays, and redirections that might at times make us feel directionless. We look at the map, but we hold our plans loosely, knowing they are prone to change. For no matter how grand and detailed the map is that we see today, it is but a small speck in God's wide and infinite galaxy of what is possible. But no matter how overwhelming the unknown can be, in grace we can breathe deep and trust that not knowing it all is okay. We will still learn what we were meant to learn. We will still grow how we were meant to grow.

Practice Peace by Noticing Other People on the Journey

Through trusting, we learn to slow down. And in that slowing down, we discover that we're not the only ones on this path. We're not the only ones trying to find our way. Sometimes simply realizing this can bring a great deal of comfort. Noticing that others are asking just as many questions as we are can reveal that in a million ways, we're learning to pace our way through, together.

Leave Room for Redirection

One of the ways we can leave room for redirection is to remain flexible. This can be a challenge because we want to get things done. We want to make progress. At the same time, we learn from nature that everything has its own natural pace. We can't slow down the movement of the wave, and we can't speed up the butterfly's metamorphosis. We can't redirect the path of the rainstorm or the snowstorm. What we learn from inclement weather is this: be prepared and also be flexible and willing to adjust. In doing so, we learn to trust that no matter the outcome, we can embrace the natural rhythm of each day.

THE PRACTICE

THE MAP

Look at a map (either a physical or digital one). Pick a road and follow it to its end. From there, find a nearby road and do the same thing. When you reach the end of that road, find another and follow it once more. Notice how there's no finish line to a map. Notice how even when you reach one road's end, the map seems to keep going. There are a thousand ways to carry on.

GROWING

CHAPTER 19

GROWING

In my full-time music days, we would often play for younger crowds. And by younger, I mean elementary-school-age children. Often the children would gather around the stage and sit on the floor while their parents sat in chairs behind them. Usually, the kids' response to my music was as one might expect: a lot of wiggling and chatting among themselves, and occasionally they would sing or clap along. One time I was setting up the next song, which was about overcoming life's challenges. I looked down and noticed that quite a few kids were still listening. As I talked, I thought, "These kids are actually listening. How do I talk to them about overcoming? They're so young . . ."

When I spoke to crowds of mostly adults, I would typically talk about the situations that most adults have lived through—disappointment, fear, some kind of loss. But with these kids, who were somehow paying attention to me, I asked, "So, who here has made it through kindergarten?" The kids grew silent, and nearly every hand shot up. "Who here has made it through first grade?" The kids who had survived first grade grew even more enthusiastic, and the enthusiasm grew louder and louder until I stopped at third grade.

"Third grade was a lot of work, huh?" I asked.

"Yes!" every fourth grader and above shouted. As the adults behind them chuckled, I kept going.

"What about second grade? First grade? Kindergarten? Were those a lot of work too?"

Every kid exclaimed, "Yes!" with many of them breaking off to chat about their experiences among one another.

"You guys have come so far. This song is for you."

I don't remember much of what happened after that because I couldn't stop thinking about the fire these children brought when sharing the news of their earnest accomplishments. The pure energy of their enthusiasm lit up the room in a way I had never seen in rooms of grown-ups who had made it through far more complex circumstances. As we get older, making it through second grade is no longer a big deal. Turning ten years old is not the massive shift it used to be. Time passes us by, and we forget all that we have already achieved. The unfulfilled dreams sing louder than the ones that came true. The unfinished projects leave more of a mark than the finished ones. We forget about all the little ways we've grown. We forget everything we've learned along the way.

The enthusiasm of these children reminded me of how capable we are of acknowledging—taking in, and also breathing out—how far we have come, honoring growth in its smallest forms.

I think embracing the act of breathing as real progress is hard because we've been trained to see smallness as inferior. Small progress doesn't make the news. Small progress doesn't earn any social media likes.

Listening to young people is a great way to be reminded of the importance of every stage of growth and how we can learn from it.

I once saw someone on the internet say, "I refuse to read a book written by someone who isn't even thirty yet." I read that comment at age twenty-one, and with total transparency, I will tell you that I held on to those words much longer than I should have. I wondered for a long time if this person on the internet, whose name and face I never saw, received some magical wisdom at thirty that I would someday have. Maybe when I was close to thirty, I might finally feel qualified.

A few months short of my thirtieth birthday, I was at an event with an author and speaker whose books I had read. He turned to me and a group of other writers and speakers in their twenties and said, "Someone once told me: don't write a book until you're forty."

"Well, so it continues, I guess," I thought, thinking about my poetry book that would be released into the world a week and a half before my thirtieth birthday.

Maybe it's just me, but I want to see more shelves filled with books written by children and teenagers. With every year in grade school, we make progress. We gather wisdom. It's easy to forget that wisdom finds us at every age. Kids say all kinds of funny, silly things, and at the same time there is an honesty in their voices that we lose as we get older. A full-bodied presence is hidden in their awkwardness. And maybe there's even something to learn from teenage moodiness, a sensitivity rising up through a young person who hasn't perfected that forced smile to try to convince everyone that everything is okay.

I am reminded of poet June Jordan's words on the young: "If we will hear [children], they will teach us what they need; they will bluntly formulate the tenderness of their deserving."[1]

There is a tenderness to the heart of the young, open to explore. Soaking everything in, always learning.

A lot of my favorite teachers are poets and philosophers who left this earth long before I was born. Their legacies were engraved in the stone plates of history before I ever learned their names. And yet, as I watch my toddler stop in his tracks, in awe of the water sprinkler, I am convinced that there is wisdom to be found at every stage of life.

To my young friends, please don't wait. You're young, and yes, you will tell this story of your life in a different way as you get older, but I promise, right here, right now, you have something to say. You are free to practice peace in public. Use your voice now. Talk about what you've learned and how far you've come. You might have a perspective now that you might not have in a decade. It's worth sharing. It's worth tapping into those challenging and awakening winds of truth blowing your way right now. Reach out and grasp. Wisdom is here. Take it in. Breathe it out. Let this be your practice.

By Growing, We . . .

Practice Peace by Breathing through Every Stage of Life

The great thing about getting older is that you don't lose all the other ages you've been.
—Madeleine L'Engle

Just by making it through the early years of school—your preteen years, teen years, and so forth—you have already been countless versions of yourself. As we get older, we forget how much harder the second semester of third grade was than the first and how distinctly different it feels to turn ten versus turning twelve. We forget all the little ways we changed and grew over the years and how each stage and phase brought its own favorite songs and dislikes, audacious hopes and hidden fears. We may not be able to remember them all, but we can know this: all these experiences informed who we are. Find peace in knowing that all along you've been growing in wisdom, courage, and grace, even if it felt like an awkward teenage phase at the time. Even if you're still learning to embrace how far you've come, you're on a journey. You've already been learning how to breathe through every stage of life.

Practice Peace by Having Empathy for Those Younger Than Us

By acknowledging the beauty and courage of our own youth, we can see the beauty and courage in other young people as well. Our stories and struggles may not be the same, but we can remember how it felt to be young, facing unknowns. We can remember how differently it felt to engage with adults who were patronizing and condescending versus those who were empathetic and treated us with dignity. And then, as we grow older, we can become those adults. Having empathy for the younger generation looks like going out of our way to let a young person know we see them because we know what a difference it made when someone saw us.

Accept Aging as a Natural and Beautiful Part of Life

We can't separate growing from aging. Growing means becoming older, which at times can be hard to accept. Sometimes we might have regrets about what we didn't accomplish or achieve when we were younger. And for all the biases against young people, there are just as many biases against getting older, and they can cause us to feel as though we are somehow worth less simply because we are aging. Because we are surrounded with advertisements and entertainment that tend to portray aging in a negative way, it takes work to see the process of getting older as not only natural but beautiful. If it feels hard to accept the wrinkles and gray hairs, that's because it is hard. But we do not become less valuable as we age. We become more of who we are only as we grow.

THE PLANT

Find a plant outside or within your home. It could be anything from a houseplant to a small shrub along the sidewalk at work. Take a picture of it, and then take another picture around the same time the next day. What slight changes do you notice? Is the light hitting the plant in a different way? Or does the plant seem to be in a new position? Some plants will move more than others, but one thing remains true: even in the smallest ways, each plant will shift, change, and grow. How are you shifting, changing, growing?

BECOMING

CHAPTER 20

BECOMING

I don't remember all their names, but I have vivid memories of the mountains I have visited. I've stood there imagining what they might say if they could speak. What do they know about stillness that we as humans never will?

Now, when I speak of my love for mountains, I am not talking about hiking them. If you notice, my descriptions of the mountains and all that surrounds them come from ground level. I personally haven't found it inside myself to put on multiple layers of clothes, thick boots, and a scarf the size of a small blanket so I can hike the mountain at three o'clock in the morning for a view of the sunrise from above.

When I speak of mountains, I speak of my love of their immovable bold presence amid all that changes in everyday life. Their jagged edges stretching up to the heavens, almost as though they defy gravity. The grassy terrain laced through the slopes, the cascading trees peeking out along the ridges, and the waterfalls carved within them that I can't see but I can feel. I speak of their superiority, their greatness. They can't be ignored or hidden.

Over the past few years, I've had the honor of sharing the stage with people I look up to, artists and authors whose music and books carried me through life's uncertainties. There's a circular feeling to this experience. Somehow it feels as if I'm going right back to where I started. Their words gave me courage because they made me feel as though I was encountering someone who had brushed up against greatness, someone who had been in the presence of many mountains.

Now, I've used the terminology "look up to" to describe those I admire, because that's the common phrases to explain the connection I've had with these people. However, what I have found is that in those moments when I've been able to meet someone I look up to, a shift happens: I go from "looking up *to*" to looking *across*. I go from admiring them on a pedestal to finally seeing that the greatness I see in them is also within me.

Just because I haven't had the success they've had, who's to say I am any less? Who's to say I have to spend another moment holding my breath because I don't see myself as "accomplished"?

Being "accomplished" by society's standards is not the requirement to do great work. Being successful in other people's eyes is not what allows us to encounter greatness. What allows us to encounter greatness is by being among God-made mountains, knowing that the same breath that breathed those mountains to life breathed life into us too.

Greatness is not restricted to the highest mountains, nor are they reserved for the people who climb them. We get to encounter greatness because of the life that has been breathed into us. It is possible for us to encounter greatness right here, where we are.

Living in Arizona, I am surrounded by the most glorious mountains every day. But what drove me to these desert mountains was not wonder and curiosity. It was a worldwide pandemic that caused us to leave California so we could save money after our business took a hit. And yet as my husband and I traveled east over the Colorado River under the desert's summer sun with our one-year-old son, God spoke to me through the mountains as they whispered, "You are in the presence of greatness."

I think we have to humbly learn that we are in the presence of greatness before we can understand what it means to have greatness within. We have to accept that the feeling of being too small against the height of the mountains is an invitation to keep looking up. The open landscape, even the desert one, is a reminder to keep looking beyond. It is necessary to understand that we are just a small part of something more.

As I was about to walk into Yayoi Kusama's exhibit at the Phoenix Art Museum, these words were written on the wall: "Our earth is only one polka dot among the million stars in the cosmos."[1] It was within the first few days of the museum's reopening since the start of the pandemic, and I got there as quickly as I could. I walked into Kusama's famous "Infinity Mirror Room" and stood at the edge. I couldn't walk into the room any further, as one normally would, because of social distancing guidelines. But in that moment, where I stood was enough. The widely celebrated Infinity Mirror Room is a room of lights and mirrors and, as Kusama says, reminds you that you are just a little dot amid it all.

As I stood there at the edge of this star-filled room that never seemed to end, thinking of my small-dot self, my eyes filled with tears. Firstly, I was so happy to be back in an art museum after they had been closed across the country for so long. I had been checking the website weekly, waiting for the doors to open again, ready to take whatever precautions necessary and practice whatever social distancing I needed to. And secondly, I cried because I was humbly reminded of my smallness and how beautiful and okay that truly is. I felt the weight of all the times I had pressured myself to be extraordinary, to try to outdo what I did the day before. To try to be the mountain itself before learning simply to be here, on the ground. The times I drove myself to exhaustion so I could prove that music executive wrong. The times I denied parts of myself because I was afraid of being "too much."

There, among all the tiny flickers of light, I exhaled and remembered my continual need to surrender my tendency to think I need to do more to be great.

Maybe the reason I am drawn to the mountains is because of their ability to remind me that at my smallest, I can still encounter greatness. I can still take part in it as the sunrise unfolds and know that I too am a part of this vast landscape. Greatness, unlike success, is not about the accomplishment of a particular aim or purpose but about realizing that presence alone is purposeful. A mountain in the distance does not gain purpose when we climb it. It does not have to perform a dance to be great. It isn't worried about outdoing itself the next day just because people are watching. No matter how far or close we are to the mountains, they possess beautifully, divinely created greatness. And they have lessons for me, right here where I stand.

As I stood at the roped-off part of Kusama's Infinity Mirror Room, unable to engage in the full experience, it reminded me that not needing to engage immediately can be a form of reverence. Sometimes we long to get up close, when maybe we need to be still and inhale what we can see from a distance.

My distance from the mountains was clear to me growing up in Georgia. Where I grew up, nearly every road we traveled regularly was lined with trees. I knew that beyond the trees there were horizon lines, sunsets, and mountains, but as a child, the trees felt like a hindrance. "If I could just see above them, then I could see the sky for what it really is," I would say to myself as we'd drive beneath the underpasses on the southeast side of I-285. I had this view then that greatness was always over there, headed west toward California, where I was born. What I didn't realize at the time was I didn't have to see mountains and horizon lines to know in the well of my soul that I was a part of something great. I didn't realize that trees stretching up to the sky pointed to greatness too.

The first time I ever flew into Georgia was on a flight from the West Coast into the Hartsfield-Jackson Atlanta International Airport. As the plane prepared to descend, the woman in the window seat next to me had expressed that it was her first time coming to the South. As we dropped below the clouds, she gasped in awe as she looked at the landscape unfolding beneath her. "Oh my, would you look at the trees!" she gasped in amazement. It was midsummer, and all the trees, both deciduous and evergreen, covered the ground beneath our feet like a never-ending forest. She immediately pulled out her phone and started snapping pictures—the exact same thing I did when I flew to the West Coast for the first time.

We brush up against greatness every single day in a thousand ways.

I wonder how differently I would see my life if I had a bird's-eye view of every day I have lived. More than the individual failures and mishaps, I would be able to see the whole landscape. I could look down at myself navigating through the corn maze of life one breath at a time. I would see myself make wrong turns, circling back and trying again. I would find myself taking a moment to rest in the grace that I was finding in the journey. I would also see the river carved into the landscape, the same landscape where

I was learning to pace myself. I would see mountains in the distance, constantly reminding me of what is greater.

Oh, how wonderful it would be to see all of life unfold from the sky. To see how it all weaves together, where all seems peaceful. But we must humbly accept our place here on the ground, where we must continue to practice peace. We may not live with a bird's-eye view, but we brush up against greatness every day. Compared with the mountains, we are small, but it's through our smallness that we begin to see more clearly. We can practice peace with this clarity: we are only one part of the bigger picture.

When we accept our smallness, and how small our inhales and exhales are in this larger picture, we start to realize that breathing through our days is possible. We start to realize that to practice peace is a lifelong journey, but we are well on our way, every single day.

In my own life, I have learned that God breathes life into my smallness, and I experience greatness from the inside out. And I will continue to tap into that greatness as I journey on through breath cycles and, thus, the cycle of life:

> To know that I am great and
> I am small all at once is to experience
> the wholeness of who I truly am.
> I have been breathed into existence,
> and I also come up from the dust of the earth
> and return as the dust of the earth.
> The world is quiet at night and yet I feel so alive.
> The world moves quickly in the morning,
> rushing the day along as I move slowly.
> It's all in the dance. It's all in the beautiful
>   combination of it all.

This is what makes it a symphony.
All the pieces are great and small.
Careful and reckless all at once.
Daring within the frame.
Wanderer within the confines of gravity.

—JOURNAL ENTRY, JULY 2, 2019

As We Continue to Become, We . . .

See the Interrelationship between Greatness and Smallness

We are small and great at the same time. We are small because we are only one human being, one blade of grass, one polka dot. But that one polka dot is a part of a greater picture, and we are a part of that greatness. I think this dichotomy is why it's possible to be humble and proud at the same time—humbled that here you are, on the ground, playing one small part in life, but proud that you are able to be a part of a larger story with everyone else too. This is why we can experience both the ordinary and extraordinary on the same day. Why God can feel incredibly close and incredibly far away. Why we can look up to a sky filled with a billion stars and somehow feel small yet someone valued as an important part of this vast universe. We are both unique and average. We live with the tension of both smallness and greatness every day, and both are a part of continuing to become who we were meant to be.

Embrace the Cycle of Growth

When we remember that life happens in cycles, sometimes we may ask, "Well, is there anything to look forward to?" This is a fair question because moving upward and onward seems like the way to go. The word *becoming*, for me at least, feels close to words like *blooming* and *rising*. It feels like something that will finally bring me to peace. But *becoming* means "the passing into a state"[2] or "any process of change."[3] These definitions remind me that we are forever just passing through from one stage to the next, and this is the act of becoming. At some points in the cycle, we will be moving upward, but if everything doesn't continue in a linear direction, that doesn't mean we are failing. At every stage, as long as we are breathing, we are becoming.

Recognize How Far We've Come

For decades, children have been known to sit in the back seat of a moving car asking their parents this famous question: "Are we there yet?" As someone who remembers asking this question quite a bit myself, I can say that it comes from a place of focusing on how far we have to go instead of how we've come. In that moment, I don't care about the miles traveled. I'm just interested in the (hopefully) smaller number of miles we have left to travel.

When we grow up, we stop asking the "are we there yet" question from the back seat of the moving car, but we don't stop asking this question about life. We turn our focus to the miles ahead of us, forgetting about all the ones it took for us to get here.

There is nothing wrong with looking ahead, but we must never forget all the miles it took to get to this place. We must never forget that while we wait to encounter greatness at some destination, we encountered greatness when we took our first breath. And then we took the next one. And the next one. Each one a small miracle of life all its own.

Whenever we ask, "Are we there yet?" when it comes to the great things we hope lie around the bend, through reflection we discover that we've encountered greatness all along the journey.

We've lived in cities and met people who have helped shape us into who we are today. We've taken in sunsets and rainstorms, and we've let out early morning laughter and late-night prayers that have all been a part of making this a life worth living. And when we take a moment to breathe in this reality, we discover that it's the greatness we encounter along the way that prepares us for the greatness up ahead.

THE PRACTICE

THE SEED

Find a seed of any kind. A mustard seed from the cabinet will do, or even the seed from a piece of fruit you've recently eaten. Hold it in your hand. Think about everything this seed could become. Ask yourself, "Is this seed something great or something small?"

HOPE

CHAPTER 21

HOPE

Many years ago I had a recurring dream. Within the dream, I would open my eyes to discover that I was slowly drifting above my bed, upward toward the ceiling. As I got closer to the ceiling, I would suddenly become aware of a hard surface under my back. I would turn and look beneath me, discovering that I was on a type of hard, bright-yellow plastic that looked like a sled of some sort. In real life, I've never been on a sled, but in the dream, this sled was familiar to me. When I suddenly realized it was there beneath me, carrying me toward the ceiling, I would think, "Oh yeah, the sled is here. I'm fine."

As my body, lying flat on the yellow sled, drew closer to the ceiling, I would feel as though I was picking up force. I thought that maybe I would burst through the ceiling and into the night sky. I started to think of all that was possible on this sled. What it might be like to see the city from above. What new world might await beyond the stars.

With every thought, my heart would race more and more, and as I got closer to the ceiling, it seemed more and more possible— maybe I would break through and shatter the ceiling. But every night as my belly came within a millimeter of touching the ceiling, gravity suddenly found its way back into the room, and just like that, I rapidly dropped from the ceiling back toward the bed.

Just before I hit the bed, the sled would magically dissolve, and I would wake up out of breath, feeling as though I had literally fallen from the ceiling.

I've lost track of the number of nights I had this dream. Every time, I recognized the sled beneath my body at precisely the same moment. The sled was always yellow. I always believed it was possible that I could go bursting through the ceiling.

I haven't had that dream in years. I've even tried to make myself think about this dream right before sleep in hopes that I could dream it again, but with a different outcome. I frequently think about this dream whenever I get on an airplane and we're on the runway, getting ready to take off into the sky.

A plane's ability to take off into thin air and be sustained there is the closest I feel to breaking through the ceiling. I hold my breath as I feel the full effect of what didn't seem possible all that long ago. For so long, the idea of humans soaring through the sky was just a dream. And now here we are.

This to me is the thrill of hope.

Hope is active imagination.

Hope is the way you look forward to the future.

Hope is grounds for believing that anything is possible.

Peace is possible.

And that is why to practice peace, I believe we must keep hope alive.

When I think about hope and the future, I think about imagination. The reason why we need imagination is that while peace brings us here, to the present moment, imagination pushes us to think beyond what we see and touch. This is why hopeful imagination is so powerful. Right here, where we are, we have the agency to pursue peace and continue to grow. To actively ask questions about the kind of future we would like to know. And not only for ourselves and our loved ones but also for the future of our communities and the world.

Like me, you have probably felt the woundedness of the world. You have witnessed the tragedies and losses that have us speechless and scrambling for solutions. You have asked, "When will we ever know peace?"

As we practice peace in daily life, we will continue to find ourselves living this question. From the time you began this book up until now, new events have likely taken place in the world that may have caused you to ask that question again. This is why I want to leave this book with a note of hope. Hope that we will continue to imagine what is possible, working through the tension and unanswered questions one day at a time. Hope that is unafraid to imagine as we breathe through this life, one moment, one headline, one question, one year at a time.

The way we do this is by regularly asking hopeful, imaginative questions with humility:

What if we tried this?
What if we tried that instead?
What if we asked these people whom we haven't
    heard from?
What if we put energy into this?
What if we tried a different approach?
And what if . . . it worked?

Asking these questions for all the issues we face today will take a lot of energy, and many will want to give up. Some will say, "What's the point of even trying?" They will speak up from the pain of their own unresolved wounds, and cynicism will shake its way to the surface. But when the weight of the world is overwhelming and we find ourselves sinking into that kind of thinking, this is what we must remember:

We need to breathe through this life one day at a time.

We can't do the work if we try to do everything at once.

We need each other.

We can have hope while also knowing we must give every effort to continue to stir hope in the collective. And the only way we're going to be able to do that is if we actively practice peace. Unless we take time to rest and grow in wisdom and grace, how will we be able to carry on every day? Unless we slow down and breathe through each day, how will we be able to finish our part of the race well, so we can pass the grace and wisdom on to the next generation?

We do not know where our hope will lead us. We do not know how long of a shadow we will cast as the sun beams down on us. But we can trust that throughout time, there will be room for peace. We can push into the uncertainty and keep going anyway. As Austin Channing Brown said, "This is the shadow of hope. Knowing that we may never see the realization of our dreams, and yet still showing up."[1]

Whether we are navigating how we will care for our planet, human rights issues in our country, or tending to the unspoken hurt in our communities and questions raised in our homes, we have to continue to imagine that better is possible. We have to imagine what it would look like if we worked through this one day at a time, together.

Hope is a radical way of looking at the past and the present and figuring out how to take a deep breath and say, "We can be better. And we will. We may not always be the best or do everything right, but we are fully engaged in the practice of pursuing peace with every single breath we breathe." Hope is realizing that a dream is more than a dream. Hope is a way of living so that dreams of love, unity, and healing can become a reality—not perfectly or easily and certainly not quickly, but all in grace. Always in grace.

In 1996, at six years old, I stood on the top of Stone Mountain. I witnessed my father become the first Black man to speak at the annual Easter sunrise service there. The title of his sermon was "To Be Continued." On that cold spring morning, we not only were a part of history but also stood on the shoulders of a dream realized—the dream Martin Luther King Jr. spoke of in his famous 1963 "I Have a Dream" speech: "Let freedom ring from Stone Mountain of Georgia."[2]

We stood on that very mountain, on Cherokee and Muscogee Creek land, where the Ku Klux Klan had rebirthed itself at the turn of the twentieth century. On November 28, 1915, the *Atlanta Journal-Constitution* wrote of their gathering: "Impressive services at the past week were those conducted on the night of Thanksgiving at the top of Stone Mountain."[3]

We stood there at dawn.

And as songwriter Patty Griffin said when she wrote "Up to the Mountain," inspired by Dr. King, "I could see all around me . . . everywhere."[4]

And at that moment, I was free to breathe in the open air. I was free to take in the moment and rest as we prepared for the rest of the journey. It has taken a few decades to find the words, but in that moment, I knew. I knew I had to keep inhaling and exhaling, my heart bent toward hope.

Dawn itself reminds me to exhale. A recurring theme in my present daydreams is sunrises, particularly the ones you see from an airplane. High above the landscape we tread on each day, the sky is widened and open with possibility, filled with too many colors to name.

Once I was on an airplane in a window seat, somewhere around 15A, when the pilot announced overhead, "Good morning, everyone! Check out this sunrise over here on our left . . . it's extra glorious today."

For whatever reason, I didn't look out at the sunrise itself that day, but instead, I turned around in my seat just in time to see everyone behind me lift up their windows, almost as if on cue. Window by window, I saw a bright-yellow glow find each person's face. As some wiped sleep from their eyes and others pulled out their phones, I saw faces of every kind all looking in the direction of the morning sun. In that brief moment, there was a togetherness that would never be again. To me, it felt like hope. To me, it felt like permission to exhale as I imagined a world where more humans could experience moments like this together.

I shared this experience on a podcast recently, to which the interviewer, referring to my art and poetry, said the kindest thing that I will always hold on to: "Morgan, you're the pilot telling us to open our windows and watch the sunrise."[5]

I took a minute to do nothing more than take in that compliment. I have never been more silent on a podcast than I was in that moment. I thought about all the poems I had written and the art I had created up until that point, and it suddenly made sense why this moment stood out to me so much. I know what it means for peace to feel far away. I know what it means to lose hope that there will be room for me to breathe freely amid everything I struggle with. I also know what it means to encounter peace beyond understanding and be left with nothing else but the conviction that I must pass it on. I must pass on every little ounce of my peace practice. It's still taking shape. There's a lot I still don't know and will continue to learn. But I know this: life has been breathed into me, and that alone sends me free into the wild of any new unknown, knowing that if I can inhale and exhale my way through, that matters. I am practicing peace.

I want everyone to have their yellow-sled-like dream that gives them the audacity to think they can shatter the ceiling. I want people everywhere to experience the golden beam of the sun on their skin at dawn. I hope for everyone's sake that we can wake up from our dream of peace and discover that together, as we inhale and exhale, peace is possible.

THROUGH HOPE, WE . . .

Keep an Active Imagination

> *Why, sometimes I've believed as many as six*
> *impossible things before breakfast.*
> —LEWIS CARROLL, *ALICE IN WONDERLAND*

The more we must face the realities of the world, the harder it is to keep an active imagination, which is all the more reason to go out of our way to do so. I believe one of the ways we can foster an active imagination is by keeping things around us that remind us of times in our lives when we had a more active imagination. I like to keep quotes around, including favorites from books I read as a child. I write them out in my personal bibliography, and I also scribble them on individual pieces of paper and leave them around. I also keep crayons around, not only for my child but for me too. Even if we don't use these items every day, having the old guitar in the corner or the board games out in the open is a visual reminder of the childlike imagination that's still possible even as life gets more complicated. For a better future, we need more imagination, not less. We need more people who are willing to drill holes in the floor, put paintings on the wall, and set the table to create breathing room for others.

Give Ourselves Permission to Dream

The difference between dreaming and imagination is that imagination is a conscious effort to create an image in our minds after being inspired. While dreams can be inspired, they usually happen on an unconscious level. This is an important distinction because while we *use* our imaginations, dreams can feel passive. Many of us don't remember our dreams from the night before, if we had them at all. We talk about a "dream" in the daytime as either a daydream or a fleeting hope of something that may never happen. But what if there is more to dreams than we can see? What if dreams could be reflections of what's stirring in the soul? What it dreams had value even if we couldn't make sense of them right away? What would happen if we gave them more space?

I am still trying to make sense of the recurring yellow sled dream, and I probably will continue to try for as long as I live. And I have daytime dreams that I'm still trying to make sense of too. I have dreams of owning land somewhere far away from the city where people can come to make art, write, and rest. I have dreams of having conversations—beyond social media comment sections—about racial reconciliation. I dream of library cards that are designed as passport booklets and you can get stamps for all the different stories and genres you discover in your reading life.

These are dreams I do not yet have comprehensive plans for. I do not know how to purchase land. As passionate as I am about real-life conversations, the process of organizing in-person events is not a strength of mine—I literally plan only one birthday party for myself per decade for this reason. I don't know a single thing about designing library cards or how it would practically work to have a library card that looked like a passport booklet. However, I will continue to dream these dreams out loud, and I hope you do too.

I want this for each of us because I believe two things are possible: One, our dreams are worth paying attention to even if we don't feel like they are practical. Even if we don't have the know-how to bring it to life, it's still worth allowing that dream to stir within us. When we see acts of peace in the world, often they began with someone's dream. Dreams don't have to be practical at first to lead to justice, reconciliation, and restoration. Before anything else, we must create room to allow ourselves to dream, especially when we are dreaming with a hope for peace. And two, you never know who out there might help you bring that dream to life. There might be a dream you have for your community right now, and someone across your city has the know-how to make it happen. Or maybe just by giving yourself permission to dream and sharing your dreams, you inspire other dreamers around you. And together, we create a world where hope is active and peace is possible.

Believe Peace Is Possible Not Only for Ourselves but for All

Many things happening in the world today might make us ask, "Is peace actually possible?" We can't seem to agree on the simplest things, so how on earth will we agree on how to pursue peace? These kinds of questions can send us inward, causing us to wonder how we can *personally* find peace even though everything else is in chaos. What we have to remember is that because peace is a practice, it can take time. While we often have to wait to see peace come to life, sometimes it is worth working toward, day by day, breath by breath. We must be willing to sow seeds of peace, even if it takes generations.

The cry for the freedom to vote in Selma, Alabama, was heard loud and clear far beyond the Edmund Pettus Bridge, over the Alabama River. The pursuit of freedom from slavery went far beyond the drilled holes in the floor of the First African Baptist Church and extended to the Underground Railroad and beyond. The need for freedom from the storm came with the instruction, "Peace, be still" (Mark 4:39 KJV) and traveled many miles and centuries beyond the Sea of Galilee. The pursuit of peace is the pursuit of freedom to breathe, not only for ourselves but for all. May we never give up in our pursuit of freedom. May we never stop practicing peace.

THE PRACTICE

THE CHILDREN'S BOOK

Keep some children's books on the shelf with all your other favorite books. They could be any books. Choose some from your childhood or some you've recently discovered. Commit to opening at least one children's book at least once a week. One week you might look at only the illustrations. The next week you might read the story more closely. Pay attention to anything in the book that stirs up a sense of wonder or causes you to use your imagination. Carry that childlike mindset with you throughout the day.

CHAPTER 22

PEACE IS POSSIBLE

(or Practice Peace)

Take heart, breathe deep.
Now is the time to practice peace,
the freedom to breathe
no matter where you are
or where you're headed.
No matter the present uncertainty.

Practice peace with the music helping you
slow down and feel more deeply,
take deeper breaths more often,
and remember what is good,
melodic, rhythmic reminders to seek out
the music
of life.

Practice peace with every breath cycle,
a symbolic reminder of wholeness.
It's time to see your story in a new way
and help others do the same.

Practice peace with the freedom
to do things a little differently now,
letting your yes be yes and letting your no
        be no.
Decide what you will do differently.
Name what's not for you, what you will say
        no to.
Name what is for you, what you will say
        yes to.

Practice peace with community,
knowing community looks different
season by season.
From dinner tables to bibliographies,
"your people" are everywhere,
their stories impacting you from near and far,
for you are never alone,
even when you feel you are.

Practice peace with empathy
by creating breathing room,
space for others to exhale
and their beautiful stories.

Practice peace with expression
by realizing that you have something to say.
Your story matters and is worth being shared.
Now is the time to breathe out all that you've
        been taking in.

Practice peace with conversation.
Let this be the source of inspiration.
Learn from working together
and offering a listening ear.

Practice peace with silence,
for in the quiet, there is room
for the delightfully unexpected
and accepting that it's okay
to not always have something to say.

Practice peace with rest,
honoring the natural rhythms of your body.
Resist the pressure to always be "on,"
engaging in the lifelong process of living
    unhurried.

Practice peace with grief,
recognizing that you are not designed to hold
    it all in,
even if you feel like you must be the
    "strong one."
You are free to feel what you need to feel.
You do not have to discount your losses.
You are free to honor the lives of those who are
    no longer here
and carry them with you in your heart
and learn how to breathe again.

Practice peace by letting it out,
speaking up when it's time to speak.
Recognize the importance of not staying
    silent,
never minimizing how you've been hurt,
allowing others to join you in support,
and seeking justice and accountability.

Practice peace with healing
by never putting time constraints
on the healing process,
with a heart wide open to others
who are on the healing journey too.

Practice peace by letting go
into humility,
releasing the need to be in control
and letting others take the credit,
embracing the value of collaboration.

Practice peace with a plan
that is rooted in getting to the heart of what's
    truly important,
not defined by failures and successes but by
    the love you give
and the life you live
right here in the present.

Practice peace by trusting,
by looking at the map as *one* of many ways to
    plan ahead
and then taking the path while holding your
    plans loosely.
Practice peace by slowing down to notice the
    other people on the journey
who are asking questions just like you.
Practice peace by traveling through the daily
    rhythms of life,
leaving room for redirection.

Practice peace by growing,
by breathing in the experiences that helped
    you bloom
into who you are today
and who you will continue to become.
Practice peace by giving yourself permission
to get older and wiser each year
as a natural and beautiful part of life.

Practice peace by becoming
who you were meant to be,
by embracing the interrelationship
between greatness and smallness.
Life is ordinary and extraordinary all at once.
Embrace the lifelong process of becoming
by recognizing that every small breath is a part
of something greater.
With every inhale and every exhale, you are
becoming.

Practice peace
by holding on
to every little thing that reminds you that you
are a part
of something so much greater than yourself.

Practice peace with hope
by keeping an active imagination,
allowing yourself to dream,
continuing to believe that peace is possible.

ACKNOWLEDGMENTS

First, I'd like to thank God for many things, and specifically the sunrises and sunsets of Arizona, where I live. In a time when I was mostly at home, hungry for new inspiration, it was these moments of the day that gracefully kept me looking where the Light poured in. Thanks to my husband, Patrick, who lovingly helpe d me create a space to write this book by doing everything from assembling my desk where I write to listening to me read the first (and very rough) drafts of this book out loud around the house. Thanks to my son, Jacob, whose joy, curiosity, and love brighten every space at all times of day, constantly reminding me why I do what I do.

Thanks to my parents, my sister, my brother-in-law, and my niece, whose homes I frequently traveled to while writing this book. These were homes where we shared stories (and often delicious food) regularly, keeping me grounded in ways I didn't know I needed. Thanks to my extended family and ancestors, for even when it comes to those I didn't get to meet, everything they went through and all the wisdom they gathered and passed on is a part of me and is woven into what I do. Thank you. I am forever grateful.

I'd like to say thanks to my therapist who has guided me through the journey of receiving my autism diagnosis. Finding out in my thirties that I am autistic hasn't been easy, and yet it was my therapist who helped me see it is still possible to be who I am in the world as an autistic person.

Thanks to Stephanie Smith and Carolyn McCready, whose love of words and skills of editing helped bring this book to life in ways I couldn't have done on my own. Working with my editors was such a joy and gave me the courage to carry on to the end. Thanks to the team at Zondervan, whom I have truly enjoyed working with during this process. Thanks to my friends and community of readers around the world. Thanks for generously sharing your time and your stories with me . . . I do not take it for granted. I truly believe this work is possible because of all the connections I've had the privilege of making along the way.

Thank you.

NOTES

Chapter 1: Peace Is a Practice

1. "Deep River," African American spiritual, Hymnary.org, accessed June 24, 2021, https://hymnary.org/tune/deep_river.
2. Jamie Gumbrecht, "Past Inspires Modern Solutions for Historic Black Church," CNN, October 21, 2010, https://www.cnn.com/2010/LIVING/10/21/oldest.savannah.church/index.html.
3. "Nari Ward: Breathing Flag," Queens Museum, September 14, 2017, http://queensmuseum.org/2017/08/nari-ward.
4. "The Oldest Black Church in North America: First African Baptist Church," First African Baptist Church, accessed May 14, 2021, https://firstafricanbc.com/history.php.
5. Monica A. Coleman, *Bipolar Faith: A Black Woman's Journey with Depression and Faith* (Minneapolis: Fortress, 2016), 339.

Chapter 2: Practice Is a Cycle

1. "Learning Diaphragmatic Breathing," Harvard Health, March 10, 2016, https://www.health.harvard.edu/healthbeat/learning-diaphragmatic-breathing.
2. "Relaxation Techniques: Breath Control Helps Quell Errant Stress Response," Harvard Health, July 6, 2020, https://www.health.harvard.edu/mind-and-mood/relaxation-techniques-breath-control-helps-quell-errant-stress-response.
3. "Relaxation Techniques," Harvard Health.
4. James Nestor, "The Healing Power of Proper Breathing," *Wall Street Journal*, May 21, 2020, https://www.wsj.com/articles/the-healing-power-of-proper-breathing-11590098696.

5. Encyclopedia Britannica, s.v. "Control of Breathing," accessed June 21, 2021, https://www.britannica.com/science /human-respiratory-system/Control-of-breathing#ref537186.

6. Toni Morrison, "The Reader as Artist," Oprah.com, July 1, 2006, https://www.oprah.com/omagazine/toni-morrison-on-reading/all.

7. Katherine May, *Wintering: The Power of Rest and Retreat in Difficult Times* (New York: Penguin, 2020), 68.

8. Maureen Murdock, *The Heroine's Journey: Woman's Quest for Wholeness* (Boulder: Shambhala, 2020), 4.

Chapter 3: Shadow and Light

1. Aundi Kolber, *Try Softer: A Fresh Approach to Move Us Out of Anxiety, Stress, and Survival Mode—and Into a Life of Connection and Joy* (Carol Stream, IL: Tyndale Momentum, 2020), 199.

2. "Needs Inventory," The Center for Nonviolent Communication, accessed June 21, 2021, https://www.cnvc.org/training/resource /needs-inventory.

3. "Feelings Inventory," The Center for Nonviolent Communication, accessed June 21, 2021, https://www.cnvc.org/training/resource /feelings-inventory.

4. Quoted in Arthur Power, *From the Old Waterford House* (London: Mellifont, n.d., ca. 1944), 64–65.

5. Chris Gerard, "The 50 Greatest Pop Songs of the '80s, Nos. 40–31," *Metro Weekly*, July 7, 2015, https://www.metroweekly .com/2015/07/the-50-greatest-pop-songs-of-the-80s-nos-40-31/.

6. Wendy Beckett, *The Mystical Now: Art and the Sacred* (New York: Universe, 1993), 32.

Chapter 4: Rhythm

1. John O'Donohue, *Divine Beauty: The Invisible Embrace* (London: Bantam, 2003), 67.

2. Tom Huizenga, "How The 'New World' Symphony Introduced American Music to Itself," NPR Music, November 24, 2018,

https://www.npr.org/sections/deceptivecadence/2018/11/24/669557133/dvorak-new-world-symphony-american-anthem.

3. Barbara A. Holmes, *Joy Unspeakable: Contemplative Practices of the Black Church,* 2nd ed. (Minneapolis: Fortress, 2017), xviii.

4. *Merriam-Webster,* s.v. "dissonance (*n.*)," accessed June 10, 2021, https://www.merriam-webster.com/dictionary/dissonance.

5. Jill Suttie, "Five Ways Music Can Make You Healthier," Greater Good, January 20, 2015, https://greatergood.berkeley.edu/article/item/five_ways_music_can_make_you_healthier.

6. *Alive Inside: A Story of Music and Memory,* directed and written by Michael Rossato-Bennett (United States: Projector Media, 2014), http://www.aliveinside.us/.

7. Anne Fabiny, "Music Can Boost Memory and Mood," Harvard Health, February 14, 2015, https://www.health.harvard.edu/mind-and-mood/music-can-boost-memory-and-mood.

8. "Leonard Cohen about the Meaning of Hallelujah," posted by YesItsAllaboutAll, July 23, 2015, YouTube video, 2:23, https://www.youtube.com/watch?v=cSV6_JzHbu8.

9. "Sheila E. Teaches Drumming and Percussion," lesson 2, 3:06, Masterclass, accessed July 20, 2021, https://www.masterclass.com/classes/sheila-e-teaches-drumming-and-percussion.

Chapter 6: Freedom

1. Mary Oliver, "The World I Live In," in *Felicity* (New York: Penguin, 2015), 11.

2. Nedra Glover Tawwab, *Set Boundaries, Find Peace: A Guide to Reclaiming Yourself* (New York: Penguin, 2021).

Chapter 7: Community

1. *Merriam-Webster,* s.v. "community (*n.*)," accessed June 21, 2021, https://www.merriam-webster.com/dictionary/community.

2. *Cambridge Dictionary,* s.v. "community (*n.*)," accessed June 21, 2021, https://dictionary.cambridge.org/us/dictionary/english/community.

3. Lexico, s.v. "bibliography," accessed June 14, 2021, https://www .lexico.com/en/definition/bibliography.

Chapter 8: Empathy

1. *Beyond the Visible—Hilma Af Klint*, directed by Halina Dyrschka (New York: Zeitgeist Films, 2020).
2. Rachel Corbett, *You Must Change Your Life: The Story of Rainer Maria Rilke and Auguste Rodin* (New York: W. W. Norton, 2016), 21.
3. Maria Popova, "The Invention of Empathy: Rilke, Rodin, and the Art of 'Inseeing,'" Brain Pickings, December 14, 2016, https:// www.brainpickings.org/2016/12/14/you-must-change-rilke -rodin-empathy/.
4. Corbett, *You Must Change Your Life*, 22.
5. *Cambridge Dictionary*, s.v. "art (*n.*)," accessed June 21, 2021, https://dictionary.cambridge.org/us/dictionary/english/art.
6. Jennifer Brown, "Navigating Crisis and Opportunity with Hearst's Chief Talent Officer, Keesha Jean-Baptiste," Jennifer Brown Speaks, July 15, 2020, https://jenniferbrownspeaks.com /2020/07/15/navigating-crisis-and-opportunity-with-hearsts -chief-talent-officer-keesha-jean-baptiste/.
7. Kevin Young, ed. *African American Poetry: 250 Years of Struggle & Song* (New York: Library of America, 2020), xxxix.

Chapter 9: Conversation

1. Gwendolyn Brooks, "Paul Robeson," *The Essential Gwendolyn Brooks*, ed. Elizabeth Alexander (New York: Library of America, 2005).
2. Langston Hughes, *The Collected Poems of Langston Hughes*, eds. Arnold Rampersad and David Roessel (New York: Vintage, 1995), 242.
3. Noah Goldberg, "Brownsville Tenants Say Facial Recognition Tech Is a Ploy for Gentrification," *Brooklyn Eagle*, May 1, 2019,

https://brooklyneagle.com/articles/2019/05/01/brownsville
-tenants-say-facial-recognition-tech-is-a-ploy-for-gentrification/.

4. *Coded Bias*, directed by Shalini Kantayya (New York: 7th Empire Media, 2020).

5. Virginia Woolf, *The Waves* (1931; repr., Hertfordshire, England: Wordsworth Editions, 2000), 74.

Chapter 10: Journaling

1. Joshua M. Smyth et al., "Online Positive Affect Journaling in the Improvement of Mental Distress and Well-Being in General Medical Patients with Elevated Anxiety Symptoms: A Preliminary Randomized Controlled Trial," *JMIR Mental Health* 5, no. 4 (Oct.–Dec. 2018): e11290, https://www.doi.org/10.2196 /11290.

2. Meister Eckhart, *Meister Eckhart: Selected Writings*, trans. Oliver Davies (New York: Penguin, 1994), 20.

3. Austin Kleon, *Steal Like an Artist*: *10 Things Nobody Told You about Being Creative* (New York: Workman, 2012), 130.

Chapter 11: Silence

1. Ann Powers, "The New Sounds of Protest and Hope," NPR Music, June 5, 2020, https://www.npr.org/2020/06 /05/870259123/the-new-sounds-of-protest-and-hope.

Chapter 12: Rest

1. Linda Geddes, "What I Learned by Living without Artificial Light," BBC, April 25, 2018, https://www.bbc.com/future /article/20180424-what-i-learnt-by-living-without-artificial-light.

2. Geddes, "What I Learned by Living without Artificial Light."

3. Emma Hornby, "Preliminary Thoughts about Silence in Early Western Chant," in *Silence, Music, Silent Music*, eds. Nicky Losseff and Jenny Doctor (London: Routledge, 2007), 142–43, https://

www.academia.edu/9782591/Preliminary_Thoughts_about
_Silence_in_Early_Western_Chant?ssrv=c.

4. Wendell Berry, *The Peace of Wild Things and Other Poems* (New York: Penguin, 2018), 25.

5. Sharon Reynolds, "Weekend Catch-Up Can't Counter Chronic Sleep Deprivation," National Institutes of Health, March 12, 2019, https://www.nih.gov/news-events/nih-research-matters /weekend-catch-cant-counter-chronic-sleep-deprivation.

6. Ferris Jabr, "Why Your Brain Needs More Downtime," Scientific American, October 15, 2013, https://www.scientificamerican .com/article/mental-downtime/.

7. "Vacation Time Recharges US Workers, but Positive Effects Vanish within Days, New Survey Finds," American Psychological Association, June 27, 2018, https://www.apa.org/news/press /releases/2018/06/vacation-recharges-workers.

8. Alan Fadling, *An Unhurried Life: Following Jesus' Rhythms of Work and Rest* (Downers Grove, IL: InterVarsity Press, 2013), 112.

Chapter 13: Grief

1. Jemima McEvoy, "1 in 5 Americans Lost Someone Close to Covid-19: Poll." *Forbes*, March 11, 2021, https://www.forbes .com/sites/jemimamcevoy/2021/03/11/1-in-5-americans-lost -someone-close-to-covid-19-poll/?sh=73b15872de5e.

Chapter 14: Healing

1. Kate Bowler, *Everything Happens for a Reason: And Other Lies I've Loved* (New York: Random House, 2019), 170.

Chapter 17: Planning

1. *Cambridge Dictionary*, s.v. "intention (*n*.)," accessed June 22, 2021, https://dictionary.cambridge.org/us/dictionary/english /intention.

Chapter 19: Growing

1. Quoted in Geneva Gay, "On Behalf of Children: A Curriculum Design for Multicultural Education in the Elementary School," *Journal of Negro Education* 48, no. 3 (Summer 1979): 324–40, https://doi.org/10.2307/2295050.

Chapter 20: Becoming

1. "Yayoi Kusama," Phoenix Art Museum, accessed June 22, 2021, https://phxart.org/artists/yayoi-kusama/.
2. Oxford Languages, s.v. "becoming (*v.*)," Google, accessed June 22, 2021, https://www.google.com/search?q=becoming+definition&oq=becoming+de&aqs=chrome.0.35i39j69i57j0l2j46j0l5.2415j0j7&sourceid=chrome&ie=UTF-8.
3. Dictionary.com, s.v. "becoming (*v.*)," accessed June 22, 2021, https://www.dictionary.com/browse/becoming.

Chapter 21: Hope

1. Austin Channing Brown, *I'm Still Here: Black Dignity in a World Made for Whiteness* (New York: Convergent, 2018), 180.
2. "'I Have a Dream' Speech, In Its Entirety," NPR, January 18, 2010, https://www.npr.org/2010/01/18/122701268/i-have-a-dream-speech-in-its-entirety.
3. "Klan Is Established with Impressiveness," *The Atlanta Journal-Constitution*, November 28, 1915, page 6, https://www.newspapers.com/newspage/26896473/.
4. "Up to the Mountain," track 9 on Patty Griffin, *Children Running Through*, ATO Records, 2007.
5. "Morgan Harper Nichols: Empathy," April 18, 2021, in *The Glo*, produced by Derik Mills, podcast, https://podcast.glo.com/podcast/morgan-harper-nichols-on-the-glo-podcast-empathy/.